Weekend Walks

Along the New England Coast

Weekend Walks

Along the New England Coast

Exploring the Coast
from Connecticut to Maine

John Gibson
with photographs by the author

BACK COUNTRY

Backcountry Guides
Woodstock, Vermont

First Edition

Library of Congress Cataloging-in-Publication Data:

Gibson, John, 1940–
   [John Gibson's walking the New England coast]
   Weekend walks along the New England coast : exploring the coast from Connecticut to Maine / John Gibson ; with photographs by the author.— 1st ed.
        p.   cm.
   Originally published: John Gibson's walking the New England coast. Camden : Down East Books, 1992.
   ISBN 0881505684
   1. Atlantic Coast (New England)—Tours. 2. New England—Tours. 3. Walking—Atlantic Coast (New England)—Guidebooks. 4. Hiking—Atlantic Coast (New England)—Guidebooks. I. Title.

F2.3 .G52 2003
917.404'44--dc21

                                                    2002026031

Cover photograph © 2003 by John Gibson
Cover design by Dede Cummings Designs
Interior design by Chelsea Cloeter
Maps on pages 151 and 165 by Moore Creative Design; all other maps by Lynda Mills

Published by The Countryman Press, P.O. Box 748, Woodstock, Vermont 05091

Distributed by W. W. Norton & Company, 500 Fifth Avenue, New York, NY 10110

Printed in the United States of America

10 9 8 7 6 5 4 3 2 1

Contents

III. Massachusetts

IV. New Hampshire

V. Maine

Introduction

When New England weekends finally arrive, most of us can't wait to get away. The outdoors beckon. The office is abandoned. We're instantly off to some favored destination, the sun and wind a tonic, the air fresh and intoxicating. And what better place to enjoy weekends outdoors in New England than along the splendid Atlantic coast? Five northeastern states border the Atlantic, and each offers outstanding coastal routes for the weekend walker bent on getting into the great outdoors on his or her own terms. There are, simply, few finer destinations anywhere.

Weekend Walks Along the New England Coast will guide you to 44 invigorating hikes in the coastal regions of Maine, New Hampshire, Massachusetts, Rhode Island, and Connecticut. Wherever your destination along the New England coast this weekend, this volume lets you get outdoors and choose among inviting strolls in nature preserves, national parks, mountain uplands, seaside towns, state reservations, and wildlife sanctuaries. Complete descriptions, photographs, convenient maps, and precise travel directions for reaching these attractive walks are included here for every route.

Weekend Walks Along the New England Coast aims to get you there and back again without fuss. This book will help you quickly become familiar with local terrain and conditions. As prominent 19th-century naturalist

and sportsman Henry Davis long ago observed: "You will never completely master a river swamp, or any other wooded area, unless you repeatedly traverse it, and you can not do this until you know how the land lies, what are the prominent landmarks, and what are the feasible routes to follow in exploring it." Modern-day walkers will enjoy the same advantage simply by using this detailed contemporary guide.

Engaging coastal walks sometimes hide in unexpected corners. In these pages you'll discover ample evidence of the real physical and psychological benefits of walking that lie, often unnoticed, close by. One virtue of coastal journeying is that outstanding places to walk are often discovered hidden in the nooks and crannies of a working waterfront, around serene harbors, along village lanes, or in the midst of scenic wetlands. *Weekend Walks Along the New England Coast* has been designed to lead you to the pleasures of walking in natural areas that remain undiscovered by many. And if you're a dedicated walker, this book always provides ready answers to that persistent question, *Where shall we go?*

Those who savor weekends as a time to get away from the hurry and noise of the nine-to-five world will garner a special kind of enjoyment along each trail or path described in *Weekend Walks*. A sense of separateness. Places to slow down and adopt a different, more natural pace. Hours of tranquility free for the taking. In his *Life in the Fields*, English writer and naturalist Richard Jefferies observed: ". . . you cannot walk fast very long in a footpath; no matter how rapidly at first, you soon lessen your pace, and so country people always walk slowly." Amen.

You will most often find an unaccustomed quiet on these paths, too. A sense of freedom from the bothersome aural clutter of our age. Walking in coastal places provides an escape from the growing noise pollution that assaults all of us. Canadian traveler, naturalist, and author Theodora Stanwell Fisher wrote in her *Driftwood Valley:* "This gift of quiet is one which inhabitants of the civilized world don't possess. They don't understand that impressions are far more impressive if no word is spoken."

As *Weekend Walks Along the New England Coast* confirms, wherever you travel in the Northeast, inviting, energizing coastal walks wait just beyond the pavement. Whatever your plans, at home or away, a weekend spent anywhere in coastal New England can become an occasion for a liberating stroll outdoors, for hours rich in new perspectives. Of the appeal of covering new ground, naturalist William T. Davis, himself a coastal walker, remarked in his *Days Afield on Staten Island*, "One of the chief advantages in visiting different meadows and

. . . woodland[s] is that it whets our perception; we are more on the look out . . . Probably there isn't a ten-acre woodlot, even near home, that has been thoroughly explored." And thoroughly explore you will with *Weekend Walks Along the New England Coast* in your day pack. Heightened, refreshed perception comes easily when you walk the terrain of each of New England's Atlantic states described in these pages.

Not only do coastal walks carry you over some of the prettiest ground anywhere, but to dedicated coastal strollers that terrain is accessible *all year*. The milder winter weather usually experienced along New England's salty coast means you can take to these paths whatever the month. The colder months are no barrier. As New England philosopher and inveterate walker Ralph Waldo Emerson wrote, "The inhabitants of cities suppose that the country landscape is pleasant only half the year. I please myself with observing the graces of the winter scenery, and believe that we are as much touched by it as by the genial influences of summer." Trails along the Atlantic zone tend to remain open even when cold weather, snow, and ice bring an end to inland walking. To those who've tried it, few experiences compare with ascending a coastal headland on a sharp, northeastern winter day, sun brilliant on the water, the wind up. And, as has been reliably observed, the other three seasons aren't all that bad, either.

Getting Ready

Unlike other outdoor sports, the demands of weekend walking are few. You can be ready to go in minutes. In this self-conscious culture of ours, couch-bound Americans spend billions annually on nonsensical entertainments. Getting out for a weekend stroll along the eastern shore costs nothing. As the crowd invests time and money suiting up for the doubtful activities extolled by mass media, the wiser citizen dons an old sweater or wind shell, picks up the day pack, and heads out, otherwise unencumbered, for a grand day on some coastal path. No burdensome and costly equipment here. Weekend shoreline walks require no fancy outfitting beyond good walking shoes or boots, a simple day pack big enough to carry lunch and extra clothing, and, if you like, binoculars, notebook, or camera. Fashion and the American obsession with costly equipment mean nothing. But then, we came to *walk*, didn't we?

What to take in that day pack? Carry a lightweight wind or rain shell with you even when the weather is mild and fair. Coastal weather changes quickly and, especially if you are in hill country, wind and wet can overtake you suddenly. In winter, settled weather inland may mask windier, sharper weather along the shore. In cooler seasons, the trick is to be prepared to layer your clothing, perhaps adding a heavy shirt or sweater under a wind shell as needed. These items take up little room in a day pack. In summer, light shirts and shorts are the rule, with long-sleeved garments favored for their sun protection. For walks in dense brush and marsh grass, wear long pants for more protection.

Some reluctant souls don't take to walking because "my feet hurt." Such a result isn't, of course, the fault of walking, but of the awful footgear some wear when out for a stroll. The walks described in this book do not require heavy-duty mountaineering boots. A light boot with a shallow lug sole offering a good grip is ideal. A sturdy work shoe or similar can be suitable, too. Select *leather* footgear that can be oiled or siliconed occasionally to keep water out. Contrary to advertising claims, cloth-topped boots cannot be effectively waterproofed and lack the rigidity to give your ankles adequate support.

The ubiquitous running shoes and sneakers so widely preferred don't serve well when walking in woods, marshes, or hill country. They are not waterproof and, when used to cross low ground, may wet through quickly. Ancient proverb: *Soggy footwear maketh not a pleasant hike.* As perusal of this book would suggest, rough ground, rock, and wet are likely to be encountered on a typical New England coastal walk. In fact, some of the most delightful walks are to be found in damp, stony, muddy, slippery, sandy, brushy, rocky places. You should be able to step with confidence and not constantly worry about wet feet or slipping.

Running shoes are made for paved or cinder surfaces. Despite their convoluted soles, running shoes don't grip well on wet ledge or slippery grass. Worse still, they offer zero ankle support, hardly what you want when covering rough, uneven ground. Think about it: Your footgear is your transportation system when weekend walking. Buy a sensible pair of lightweight, lug-soled leather boots with adequate ankle support, and you'll find walking that much more comfortable. Taken care of, good leather boots last for many years.

Getting Around

Most of the walks described in this volume lie close to settled areas. A few are located in more remote, wooded preserves or headlands that are distant from town. In either case walkers will enjoy the journey more by

becoming familiar with the general area in which they are hiking. Reviewing local, regional, and state charts *before you go* can add to your sense of the terrain. A number of coastal communities, clubs, and associations publish local maps that include trails in their area. Building a small, personal collection of regional maps and keeping them in a handy drawer, ready for convenient use, supports your hiking.

The maps provided in this book are simple and straightforward and will get you there every time. If you prefer maps with greater detail—for example, those that show specific topographical features or cover a wider area—United States Geodetic Survey (USGS) maps are useful. USGS "quads" are typically available at local sporting goods, backpacking, and hardware stores. Walkers should always carry a compass and know how to use it. However ironic, far more of us get lost in wooded areas near home than in the more remote, wilder backcountry of New England.

Maps serve as useful guides only if you can read what they tell you. When using the maps in this book, always note the position of the *North* arrow before setting out. Magnetic north is usually at the top of the page, and you need to orient your map with a compass so that the position of the map reflects the actual lay of the land. If you're not confident in getting about in the woods even with map in hand, consult *Be Expert with Map and Compass* by Bjorn Kellstrom, an excellent introduction to the subject available in paperback. Still, as noted earlier, the walks in this volume are generally close to settled areas, and trail routes can be followed easily. So if you're unfamiliar with woods walking and following route directions, don't let that deter you. Get out on the trail and learn as you go, perhaps with a more experienced companion. With a compass in your pocket and the maps in this book, you will find your way without difficulty.

An Etiquette for Weekend Walkers

The walks described in this volume lie mainly in public lands or in private preserves where walking is encouraged. In a few cases trails may cross other private grounds, sometimes close to dwellings. You're urged always to walk with consideration wherever you hike, showing courtesy and respect for the privacy and rights of landowners on whose property, by dint of customary use, these trails are kept open. If you inadvertently drift from the path and find yourself walking through someone's dooryard, it's never untimely to stop and ask permission to do so, paying your respects to the owner. Most people appreciate this, and some will also prove helpful, offering directions and waving you on through. It's only through mutual consideration and courtesy that these walking paths can be kept open with continuing access for all.

Using This Guide

Each weekend walk in this book, regardless of location, contains clear directions for reaching the trailhead. Be observant. Some parks and reservations have opening and closing hours. It's worth calling ahead. Sometimes road signs or landmarks change or are removed. Access roads may be blocked or seasonally gated. Don't hesitate to stop and ask for directions locally.

Trail descriptions in *Weekend Walks Along the New England Coast* will give you a real sense of what to expect as you walk, and will point the way as you move at your own pace through the countryside. The text comments on changes in route direction as needed. Interesting natural features and any unusual terrain or hazards are also described. Refer regularly to this book's descriptive features, and you'll enjoy your walking hours even more. Keep this guide in your pack, not back in your car.

One of the enduring pleasures of weekend walking in New England's coastal region is sampling the unique flavor of coastal terrain in each state from Connecticut to Maine. Every state is different, shoreline geography and topography varying with each region and state. From the quiet, accessible, wooded shores of southern New England to the rocky, bold headlands of Maine, variety is a fact of shoreline life, and this variety adds spice to each weekend away.

A case could be made that the coastal region, from southern Connecticut to downeast Maine, is really a state unto itself, salty, unique, wedded to a world unfamiliar to inlanders. In his *Galapagos: World's End*, ecologist, explorer, and writer Charles William Beebe noted: "A first walk in any new country is one of the things that makes life on this planet worth being grateful for . . ." That salutary feeling, the timeless pleasure of setting out for new territory close to home or farther afield, is precisely what this volume supports. Enjoy the walk.

I. Connecticut

1 • Lucius Pond Ordway Preserve (Devil's Den)

Location: Weston, Connecticut
Distance: 1 to 3 miles (depending on route selected)
Walking time: 1 to 2½ hours

For Nutmegers in search of a cache of weekend walks in one sublime pocket of quiet woodlands, the journey to Devil's Den is an obvious choice. Officially dubbed the Lucius Pond Ordway Preserve and formerly owned by the late Katharine Ordway, Devil's Den is today a superb natural reservation controlled and managed by The Nature Conservancy. The original preserve, host to a range of environmental and conservation programs, contained 1,540 acres. In 1990 another 85-acre parcel was added by the town of Weston. Not 50 miles from New York City, Devil's Den offers days of pleasant walking on more than 15 miles of secluded trails in mixed, wooded terrain.

Home to dozens of bird species, the Ordway–Devil's Den acreage is the site of new local studies of breeding populations. The worm-eating warbler and the imperiled wood thrush are two of the seasonally resident species recently studied. These and other birds that summer in southern Connecticut and winter in the neotropical regions are being observed to measure breeding success and population trends.

Red fox, muskrat, gray squirrels, cottontails, and other animals live in the preserve lands. Devil's Den also boasts an interesting variety of terrain. A mix of deciduous forest, swampland, ledgy upland, and streamside pathways, the preserve lists more than four hundred plant species and a variety of woodferns, shrubs, and trees. A series of short guides to wildflowers, ferns, shrubs, and trees have been published at $4.00 each and are available by mail from: Devil's Den Preserve, The Nature Conservancy, P.O. Box 1162, Weston, CT 06883. They will add to your enjoyment of a visit here.

Leave I-95 at Westport where the interstate crosses US 1 to reach the trails at Devil's Den. Take US 1 *south* through Westport and *turn west* and northwest onto CT 57 from the village center. Follow this road to the cluster of shops in Weston, where it runs *north* from town together with CT 53. Stay on CT 53 and go through a yellow flashing light just under a mile north of Weston. Two and one-half miles north of the village, *go left* on Godfrey Road and continue 0.5 mile west, making a *right* turn onto Pent Road, which leads to the preserve parking area and information board.

Take time to read the board notices and other information that will acquaint you with current programs at the preserve. Detailed maps are also available for loan here. The trail system, mostly south–north loops, consists of footpaths and cross-country ski trails that intersect at various points. Most of the trails are named, and all junctions are numbered, so you can easily find where you are on the map when you come to a trail junction marker.

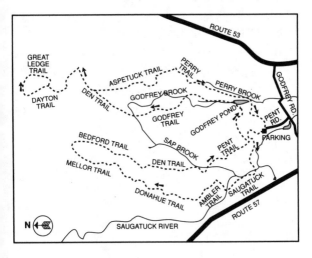

Devil's Den contains several days' worth of walks, each interesting in its own way, and each deserving your unhurried attention. Recommended:

1. A western loop of the preserve, going north and northwest on the Saugatuck Trail, the Ambler and Donahue Trails, and the Moller Trail, then returning via the Bedford, Den, and Pent Trails. This 5-mile loop climbs the knoll on the extreme west side of the park, where there are fine outlooks over the Saugatuck River and toward Ambler Gorge. The Moller and Bedford Trails follow Ambler Brook, and Sap Brook is crossed by the Pent Trail on the return.

2. A loop through the eastern and northern end of the preserve on the Harrison, Godfrey, Den, and Dayton Trails to Great Ledge. The Dayton, Aspetuck, Perry, and Laurel Trails are used on the return. This circuit passes the north shore of Godfrey Pond, goes through the central swamp of the preserve, and (on

the short Great Ledge Loop) ends at the excellent views above Great Ledge. The Perry Ski Trail leads to the south side of Godfrey Pond on the return.

Ordway–Devil's Den Preserve is open throughout the year from dawn to dusk. Since a number of the trails go through or near low ground, waterproof footwear should be worn. Carry binoculars and a field guide to plants, trees, and shrubs. More information on the preserve is available by calling (203) 226-4991.

2 · Milford Point Sanctuary

Location: Milford, Connecticut
Distance: 1 mile
Walking time: 1 hour

Here is a short, compressed walk for bird lovers on a tiny bit of shoreland in a neighborhood where the waters of the Wepawaug and the Housatonic mingle with the Atlantic. Milford Point Sanctuary offers an observation point for shore strollers who wish to observe a range of avian species and other wildlife close up. Situated next to the Charles E. Wheeler Preserve just above Stratford Point and adjacent to a colony of cottages and other structures, this reservation, encompassing sand spit and riverine marsh, provides a unique location for seeing both land and shorebirds in significant numbers. Walkers at Milford Point will observe a variety of birds aloft over grassy marshland and several tidal, barrier beaches while following the shoreline. Good views inland and to seaward add to the interest of a brief stroll here. This tiny preserve offers evidence that crucial resident and migratory bird habitat can coexist with nearby development if people work cooperatively.

Although the sanctuary lies only a few minutes' drive from I-95, a series of winding streets in residential neighborhoods must be negotiated. Leave I-95 at Exit 34, going *left* on US 1 for 0.25 mile, and then *right* on

Lansdale Avenue. Follow this street, which merges with Milford Point Road, and arrive shortly at Naugatuck Avenue. Cross Naugatuck Avenue and, later, Court Street. Continuing on, you make a bend to the *right* and, in 0.75 mile, an abrupt *left*. You next come to Seaview Avenue, where you go *right* for a few hundred yards and come to a dead end amid a jumble of cottages. A sign marks the sanctuary. Drive in to the right of the sign and proceed into the grassy parking area by an old building.

Behind the parking area, to the west through the thin line of trees, is the 800-acre-plus Wheeler Preserve. This broad plain of marshy sediment bisected by inlets and brooks shelters geese, ducks, and wading birds, which find nesting sites and good conditions for foraging in the web of the marsh. Some time spent here with a spotting scope or binoculars will be well repaid in the sheer number of birds seen.

In front of the old building by the parking area, look for a small registration bench. Current bird sightings are listed in the register. Entries from one autumn Sunday indicated how varied and numerous are the species here:

> 2 widgeons
> 2 hooded mergansers
> 1 common loon
> 5 harriers
> 3 horned grebes
> 7 common goldeneyes
> 2 red-breasted mergansers
> 3 great blue herons

Also listed on the same day's sightings were Lapland longspur, horned larks, ruddy turnstones, canvasbacks, and yellowlegs. These represent only a fraction of the

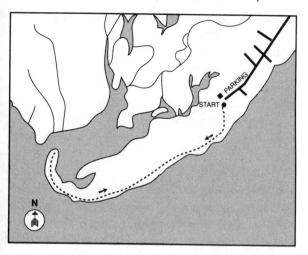

species seen at Milford Point annually. If you would like a birding list for the point and all of Connecticut, send $2.65 to: Leon Barkman, 26 West Street, Newtown, CT 06470.

To walk to the point, go southeast along the path in a grove of trees, cross a paved private road, and proceed to the shore. The shoreline arches southwest, fronted by two barrier beaches rather like sand spits. These little barrier strips create small lagoons where some of the species mentioned above take shelter. Least terns breed on the barriers, and herons wade in the protected waters. Behind you, above the beach toward the road, flattened dunes support thin concentrations of beach grass where killdeer and piping plover build their fragile ground nests.

Go right and southwest, keeping to the shoreline. Views of the extensive mudflats at the mouth of the Housatonic River open up here as you gradually work your way around to the west. Short Beach and Stratford

Point are directly across the channel. You reach the brushy, tree-lined point after a short walk beyond a row of beach houses. More time for looking about with scope or binoculars should be allowed here. With mud-flats to the west, the marshy Wheeler Preserve to the north, and the beach to the east, heavy concentrations of aquatic and shorebirds are all around you. When you leave, retrace your steps along the shore to the connecting path leading to the register board.

Since Milford Point Sanctuary (which is managed by the New Haven Bird Club) is only the narrowest strip of land in an otherwise settled area, please do not stray onto adjacent private property or roads. Grassy areas away from the water's edge should be avoided, as they contain hidden nesting sites of already pressured species. If you walk to the point in summer, carrying insect repellent is advised.

3 · Westwoods Preserve

Location: Guilford, Connecticut
Distance: 2 to 4 miles (depending on route selected)
Walking time: 2½ to 4 hours

Perched in Guilford near the coast not far north of New Haven, Westwoods is an exceptional forested oasis comprised of lands in the Cockaponsett State Forest, holdings of the the Guilford Conservation Trust and several privately owned woodlands. Abutting 500-acre Stony Creek Quarry Preserve, which itself surrounds a working quarry, this combined 1,000-acre reservation supports a network of more than a dozen intersecting trails that offer appealing walks in varied terrain. The two adjoining reservations are connected via a trail that crosses the Guilford-Branford town line, and walkers can conveniently access both preserves from a common entry. Credit for the trail network serving Westwoods' fine woodlands goes to State Service Forester Michael Pochan, who developed trails here with trail consultant Richard Elliott and members of the Guilford Conservation Commission.

Westwoods lies in a wedge of rolling countryside, with US 1 to the east and I-95 to the north. Drive to Exit 57 on I-95 and go *southeast* on US 1, otherwise known as the Boston Post Road. About 0.5 mile *south* of I-95, just before you come to Bishops Orchards, bear *right* and *west* on Peddler's Road. Follow this road a little over a mile and park in a turnout on the *left* just past Denison Road. This is the No. 2 trail entrance to the preserve. There are six in all.

A well-marked but rather confusing network of interlinked trails greets the walker. The rough map included here is adequate to get you around, but you would be well advised to purchase a more complete trail map at the Bishop's Orchards store or by sending $3.00 plus postage to: Guilford Land Conservation Trust, P.O. Box 200, Guilford, CT 06437. Trails frequently cross one another here, and it is blissfully easy to wander off one and onto another, or onto game trails. Unless you have a natural sense of direction, carry a compass with you on this walk, along with the map and this book.

You can plan a whole series of walks in Westwoods, but this one will get you started and introduce you to some of the unique features of the park. From the Peddler's Road parking area, descend south on a bit of broken pavement, dipping into an open field surrounded by mixed growth. This is the White Circle Trail, which you take past a clump of staghorn sumacs and over some rocks into the woods. With a few houses in sight above and to the left, you walk southwest through a hemlock and oak forest ringed with greenbrier. Watch for the Green Circle Trail on your left, which breaks downhill and then runs east along the northern swamplands of the park. Take this trail leftward, skirting the bog, rising and falling through groves of rhododendrons, fractured ledge, spruce, and hemlock. Red maples and dense spotted alder make the bog itself almost impenetrable to the eye, except in winter.

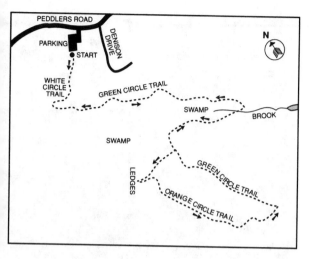

Three-quarters of a mile eastward along the swamp, the trail crosses a pleasant little brook on a wooden footbridge, then doubles back westward above the swamp in pretty forest dominated by tall hemlocks and white pines. A little farther on, the trail rises south and left toward the center of the preserve, soon crossing a trail marked with green rectangles. Go right and west on this new trail. In a few minutes you come to a junction with the Orange Circle Trail. Cross this trail briefly and take some time to explore the great, granitic hump in front of you. This large exposed dome of weathered igneous rock is interesting to climb around, and an alternate loop of the Orange Trail runs right through some of the clefts in the rock mass. This dome is one of two in the center of Westwoods and is the more exposed of the two. These outcrops of granite, part of the Stony Creek formation, are similar to those quarried nearby in the adjacent preserve in Branford.

Next, go back to the Orange Circle Trail that you crossed before. Go right and southeast on this trail through deciduous woods, dropping toward another swamp. You come to a crossover with the Blue Rectangle Trail, where you go left parallel to some power lines and, in less than ¼ mile, come to the Green Circle Trail again. Go left on the Green Circle Trail and climb steadily up the other major hummock in the preserve. You will find yourself again in tall, old hemlocks as you ascend to a point where there are views to Long Island Sound at the highest spot in Westwoods.

The return to your car is made by following the Green Circle Trail downhill and northward as it drops to the swamp and then goes east to the footbridge. Crossing the stream, go west along the swamp as before, gradually rising to the White Circle Trail by which you entered the park.

This circuit through the hilly center of Westwoods can be completed in 2½ hours. Many other trails provide diversion in the park once you get the lay of the land. From the same starting place, take the White Circle Trail its full distance to the southern limit of the preserve by pretty Lost Lake, and then go left on the Orange Circle Trail and follow it northward its full length past the Indian cave to the swamp and back to your starting place. This 4-mile loop will fully tax your hiking shoes. For other trips in Westwoods and neighboring Stony Creek Quarry Preserve, see the complete Westwoods map mentioned earlier.

Giving the complexity of the intersecting network of trails in this very large reservation, you're again reminded to always carry a map and compass when walking here.

4 · Bluff Head

Location: North Guilford, Connecticut
Distance: 1 mile
Walking time: 1 hour

Bluff Head is a steep, low promontory rising above Meyer Huber Pond in North Guilford. The outlook provides good views above the Coginchaug River drainage above Quonnipaug Lake. In fair weather the hill delivers views inland toward Hartford, the state capital, and southward to the Atlantic. Accessible highlands are rare in the Connecticut coastal zone, and an opportunity to gain the high ground and look about shouldn't be missed. This short hike over Bluff Head makes a fine afternoon's outing in spring, high summer, or autumn.

Bluff Head (not to be confused with Bluff Point State Park, described in the next chapter) lies between North Guilford and Durham on CT 77. The easiest approach is from the south, leaving I-95 at Exit 58 in Guilford. Travel *north* on CT 77 through lovely farm and river country, passing pretty Quonnipaug Lake on your right. At the north end of the lake you pass a boat launching facility. You'll find the parking area for the bluff on the *left* in a grove of pines 0.5 mile *north* of the boat launch and 8.75 miles *north* of the I-95–CT 77 junction.

The short hike to the summit of Bluff Head leaves

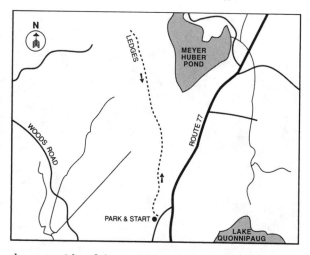

the west side of the parking area and climbs steeply uphill to the northwest under a canopy of hardwoods. If you ascend in wet weather, expect a slippery passage and use caution. Lug-soled shoes or boots should be worn whatever the season. The blue-blazed path tops out shortly and proceeds northward along a sharp escarpment above the road. Rising farther, the trail comes next to a tiny, ledgy promontory with fine views over Meyer Huber Pond to the northeast. Rolling fields lie opposite, and you can gaze over Quonnipaug Lake from here also.

The trail pulls to the west briefly through scrub oak and then winds northward to the summit lookout, where the views open up further. If the air is dry, you may be able to see the Hartford skyline, 25 miles due north. Views south range over Long Island Sound and the North Shore of Long Island itself. The effect is quite striking, rather like the tramp over Mount Agamenticus described in the Maine section of this book.

Bluff Head is a favorite spot not only for walkers but for Connecticut bird-watchers, too. The nearly 800-foot-high ridge makes an excellent spot for observing seasonal bird life and the thrilling migrations of thousands of broad-winged hawks *(Buteo platypterus)* in the last two weeks of September. According to the *National Audubon Society Field Guide to North American Birds,* "This hawk is known for its spectacular migrations; thousands of birds fly by, with single flocks of up to several hundred individuals ... Great numbers migrate along the eastern ridges in mid-September." Bluff Head accommodates, as well, a variety of resident bird species.

When you've completed looking around the summit

ledges, carefully retrace your steps to the parking lot. It is also possible, with a little exploring, to walk west off the summit and connect with a woods road that loops around the hill to the south and east, returning to the parking area. The walk to the bluff lookouts and return via the path requires about an hour.

5 · Bluff Point State Park

Location: Groton, Connecticut
Distance: 3 to 4 miles (depending on route
   selected)
Walking time: 3 to 4½ hours

Just east of New London, where the Groton Reservoir
drains southward toward Fisher's Island Sound, Groton's Bluff Point State Park occupies a rugged, unprettified point of land fronting on the Atlantic. Bordered by salt water on three sides, Bluff Point offers the walker nearly 800 acres of mixed terrain and unmixed tranquility in which to explore.

Despite being in the midst of what is usually thought of as an industrial-residential zone in the highly developed Providence–New Haven corridor, Bluff Point remains a wild, densely wooded place of little bays and inlets. You'll find a collection of routes here worthy of repeat visits. A level network of old tote roads bisect Bluff Point and make hiking easy. Walking here is pleasant in any season, but if you come in early autumn the woods are redolent of decaying leaves and grasses, and you are likely to have the ground almost to yourself at the height of the foliage season.

From north or south, approach Groton on I-95 and leave the highway at Exit 88; then proceed *south* on CT 117 for just a mile. At the intersection of CT 117 and

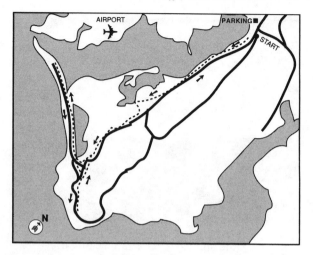

US 1, go *right* and *west* for 0.3 mile to the Groton Town
Hall, where you bear *left* onto Depot Street. This street
runs *south* under railroad tracks and, dirt surfaced, continues to the point parking area in another 0.25 mile.
Leave your car on the *right* near the inlet.

Walk past the barrier gate and head southeast and
south on a gravel road that parallels the inlet to your
right. You have good views up the water toward the
ocean from the moment you set out. (On an autumn
walk here not long ago I counted more than 20 pairs
of mute swans gliding around the inlet.) You immediately pass a road on the left; stick to the main road and
continue south. Soon the road is bordered by a canopy
of trees as the trail pulls slightly away from the inlet.
Red oak, bur oak, sassafras, red maple, black birch, and
other growth hug a wall to the right and cover the slope
to the left. Dense common greenbrier and European
bittersweet thickly entwine trees and branches. Walking on, you pass a clearing marked by a trio of oaks

standing amid another great tangle of bittersweet, which seems to flourish everywhere on the point. You pull back closer to the broad channel now and arrive at a granite barrier near the shore where the views across the protected water are excellent. Occasionally a plane lumbers into the air from the small airport beyond the channel. More swans and a variety of ducks and sea-birds rest on the water.

You pass an old orchard as you walk over a causeway abutting marshy ground and reenter the canopy of deciduous woods. Watch for a brushy side road that soon departs to the right. Take this road rightward as it leads through oak and cedar groves to a series of pretty, small inlets off the main channel. The trail moves generally to the south-southwest through increasingly dense scrub to the head of one of these inlets. If you move quietly here during migratory seasons, you are likely to spot herons, snowy egrets, and a variety of ducks. This trail intersects another that, running left and east through bayberry and black birch scrub, lets you reconnect with the main road walked earlier. A stone wall lies to the right of this junction.

Once back to the gravel road, go right, continuing south, and pass a connector road that runs uphill. Boulder outcrops and fractured ledge are seen along the road and on the rise to the left. Deer paths intersect the main road and disappear again into deep cover. The trail pulls a bit toward the southeast to a series of bluffs with fine views over Fisher's Island Sound and Long Island Sound. From the bluffs, descend westward to the distinctive sand spit that protects a marshy area and the channel you have followed. Walk the final ½ mile out to what is known locally as Brushy Point, where a narrow channel admits the open sea. Water views here are also first-rate.

The walk thus far will have taken at least an hour and a half. You may now wish to explore the boulder-strewn forehead of Bluff Point by tracing the shore southeastward past the bluffs. Another trail leaves the beach shortly and climbs the central rib of the point, working its way northward for 1½ miles and emerging near your starting point. You may wish to follow this alternate trail on the return instead of returning to the bluffs and retracing your original route out to the parking area. To make the round trip from parking area to the bluffs, out to Brushy Point, and then back via either path, it's wise to allow 3½ to 4½ hours of unhurried walking.

6 · Barn Island Wildlife Area

Location: Stonington, Connecticut
Distance: 2½ to 3½ miles (depending on route selected)
Walking time: 2 to 2½ hours

Barn Island Wildlife Area is hardly a manicured place, but rather a rough, wild collection of natural features to explore in solitude. Excellent water views greet the walker here, but the terrain consists mainly of walks through grasslands, partially wooded fields, and around small, impounded ponds and salt marsh. The preserve is a protected zone for a variety of nesting and migrating land and shorebird species. A superb area for bird observation, Barn Island demands that the walker slow down, proceed quietly, and take in, at close range, the natural texture of this place and the species that inhabit it. Barn Island gives you an opportunity to witness how a little beneficent intervention by humans in an already favorable environment can enhance the terrestrial and avian productivity of an area.

Barn Island rests just south of the Rhode Island line in Connecticut's southeastern corner. To drive to the wildlife area, take I-95 to Exit 91, *west* of Westerly, Rhode Island. Go *south* from the exit on Taugwonk Road about 0.25 mile, turning *left* onto Main Street, which you follow for 1.5 miles. Go *left* on US 1 and fol-

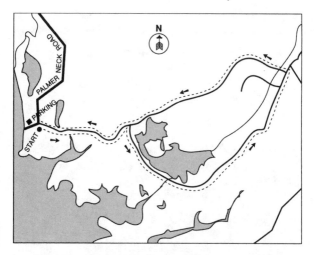

low it to Greenhaven Road. Turn *right* onto Greenhaven Road and make another immediate *right* onto Palmer Neck Road, which you travel 1.75 miles to its end. You will come to the trailhead (left) just before you reach the boat ramp at road's end. Leave your car in a small, shaded lot opposite the trailhead.

Start by walking down the road to the boat ramp. Here you'll find broad views across a cove toward the ocean. You are standing in Connecticut, but Rhode Island technically begins a short distance out in open water, for the state boundary lies midchannel. Boating activity may be hectic here in summer, and this fine outlook on the channel is best enjoyed in the other, quieter seasons. While near the ramp, take some time to inspect the cove with your binoculars for ducks and geese.

Going back up the rise to the trailhead, you walk right and eastward through mixed-growth woods on an ungraded service road that leads down to the marsh. The route now consists of a walk along the service road

past a series of water impoundments that are currently managed for ecological diversity and to attract and support avian wildlife. The impoundments may be open to tidal flushing or closed to preserve consistent water levels and lower salinity. By controlling drainage and freshwater–saltwater exchanges, biologists can create environments that favor particular plant and animal species and, to a limited extent, reduce the insect population. This section is prime bird habitat and should be walked with binoculars at the ready. The trail continues past four impoundments, with the last being the largest as you proceed east. To the south is the open cove seen earlier, and to the north lie ponds and acres of cordgrass and switchgrass punctuated with wooded bits of higher ground.

When you reach the fourth pond, you can turn and retrace your steps to the main road or continue around and make a loop through the center of the wildlife management area. If you wish to make the loop, simply stay on the dirt service road as it bends to the left and north, gradually pulling away from the impoundments and through grassy mudflats and some wooded ground. Keep your own catalog of natural attractions as you walk through the mixed cover. About ¾ mile after turning northward, you will find two side roads to the left. Take the second of these, which runs first west and then southwest, rejoining the service road between the second and third impoundment. Once you are back on the service road, go right (west) and return to the parking area.

The walk around the loop is nearly 3½ miles and can be completed in not much over two hours, but birders will want to plan to take longer. The number of bird species found here in the warmer months and during migrations is very extensive and worth patient observation. If you visit Barn Island in summer, carry strong insect repellent. As suggested earlier, binoculars or a spotting scope and a bird guide absolutely belong in your day pack on this ramble.

II. Rhode Island

7 · Napatree Point

Location: Watch Hill, Rhode Island
Distance: 3 miles
Walking time: 2½ hours

Napatree Point lies in the well-to-do little village of Watch Hill, Rhode Island. A dune-crested arc of white sand separating Little Narragansett Bay from Block Island Sound, Napatree is as far west or south as you can go on the Rhode Island mainland. Today a 1½-mile-long sand spit, Napatree Point is an outstandingly beautiful place to walk for those who love sand, sea, open bays, and birds.

History and weather have taken their toll here in a dramatic way. The point and its barrier beach are what now remains of a vastly altered landscape, every square foot reflecting the powerful shaping force of wind and water. This beach once was considerably more extensive, but the notorious hurricane of 1938 broke through the long arm of earth and sand, severing Sandy Point, which today is an island in Little Narragansett's waters. The visual impact of the storm has been captured recently in a PBS television documentary on the '38 storm system that swept New England.

This storm-wrought wreckage, occurring more than a half century ago, changed the human-made landscape, too. The ferocious hurricane winds and battering surf swept the point clear of the cottages and houses that littered the fragile neck—cottages that, of course, should never have been placed there. Of those who did not leave the point in time, many lives were lost.

The urge later, as everywhere on similar Atlantic beaches, was to build again in the same vulnerable spot. That, fortunately, has not occurred. Ironically, the storm and subsequent local conservation efforts may be responsible for the relatively pristine condition of the point today. Napatree is best visited from late September to mid-May. Those are the choicest months to escape the bane of local tourism and beach bathing, and they're also the periods of significant bird migration.

To reach Napatree Point, go to the center of Westerly, where the traffic flow circles the downtown area. Go *right* at the large, brick trust company downtown, and *keep right* at a sign that reads TO BEACHES. Drive *south* on RI 1A through Avondale and continue on to Watch Hill. This road winds among Watch Hill's mansions, and you soon drop *west* (right) on Watch Hill Road to a cluster of shops and a big parking area by the water. This spot can be forbiddingly crowded in summer, but in fall, winter, or spring you will find it pleasantly deserted.

Leaving your car in the main lot, walk west through a second lot and past some weatherworn elevated cabanas on the left. Look for a storm fence to the right that bears a sign indicating the beginning of the walk. Enter the conservation area and walk southwest on the path to the topmost point on the dunes. *Please stay on the main trail.* Dune stability depends upon the presence of fragile plant life and grasses, the roots of which prevent topsoil migration. From this vantage point you can see the whole majestic sweep of the neck of land that

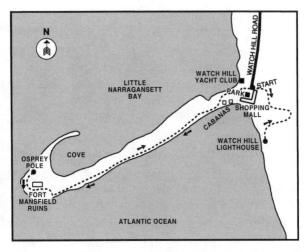

you will walk. On a sunny winter day with the wind active, the neck is like a great barrier of white light dividing the furrowed waters of the ocean from the more tranquil passages of the sheltered bay behind it.

Drop down left to the beach and commence the shore walk southwestward. The tip of the point is always ahead of you, looking, perhaps, 15 minutes away. But this is a longer walk than the eye registers, for the end of the sand is about 1½ miles away when you set out. Walking is most comfortable on the wave-hardened sand below the riprap.

The point captures the usual remnants of marine and tidal life washed up on the shore, and committed beachcombers will enjoy this aspect of the walk. But Napatree Point enjoys a kind of quiet renown as a site for exceptional birding, and there is something to observe in that department throughout the year. Rhode Island Audubon notes that the point lies in the pattern of hawk migrations in late September. (Call the Audubon headquarters in Smithfield at 401-231-6444 for current bird advisories.) Broad-winged hawks *(Buteo platypterus)* and sharp-shinned hawks *(Accipiter striatus)* are two common seasonal migrants. Northern harriers, merlins, and American kestrels may be seen as well as lesser common loons and great and double-crested cormorants. A variety of common gulls, ducks, and waders are present, too.

As you walk, the high ribs of the dunes stay to your right. They are dotted with crops of beach plum, dusty miller, and beach grass *(Ammophila breviligulata)*. Beach grass is a major factor in dune formation, for it is stimulated to grow by moving sand. Sand particles are trapped by the grass stem, and rhizomes are laid down in lattice fashion outward from the stem. The effect is to provide a dense network of roots that lace together and bind the unstable sand mass. Without the protective, interlaced system these plants supply, the fragile sandform would continually migrate, defenseless against the wind. Of course, many weeks and months of growth are required to knit together even a tiny area of the sand mass. A single, clumsy human footstep will crush, uproot, or retard this necessary growth.

At the far end of Napatree, some boulders indicate a point where you can bear right and up the rise into some low scrub to the site of Old Fort Mansfield. Overgrown with bittersweet, the ruins of this fort are a good commentary on the keenness of the military mind. This fortification was meant to guard access to Little Narragansett Bay but, upon reflection, it was reckoned that a fort on a neck was indefensible. Attackers could secure the inland side of the neck and then sit quietly, starving out the garrison. What remains of this by-no-means

unique folly provides good views back into the protected bay and to nearby posts where endangered ospreys nest in-season. Some further exploration of the rocky terminus of the point is possible (with caution) beyond the fort. When you are ready, retrace your steps to the parking area.

A short side trip can be made up the road to Watch Hill, and thence down a side road past some gingerbreaded old houses to attractive Watch Hill Light. Allow at least 2½ hours to make the trip out to Napatree Point and back, including the optional hike up to the lighthouse.

8 · Ninigret National Wildlife Refuge

Location: Charlestown, Rhode Island
Distance: 1 to 3 miles (depending on route selected)
Walking time: 1½ to 2½ hours

Charlestown is home to the long, slowly decaying runways of what once was an important naval air station. Old taxiways are slowly crumbling, giving way to grass and brush, and the planes are, of course, long gone. Something marvelous has come of all this: A developed zone is opening up to more natural uses. Walkers are returning to explore the territory. In an era when so much undeveloped land has beern despoiled for one doubtful purpose or another, the Ninigret Wildlife Refuge has become that rarest of things, developed land reverting to its original, wilder uses. Away from the crumbling pavement here you'll find 400 acres of woodland and marsh just a stone's throw from the Atlantic. Located between Westerly and Kingston, Ninigret makes a fine destination for walkers ready to explore this newly available ground.

Ninigret can be reached via US 1 and is located a few miles *southeast* of Charlestown center. The entrances to the two sections of the reserve described here are

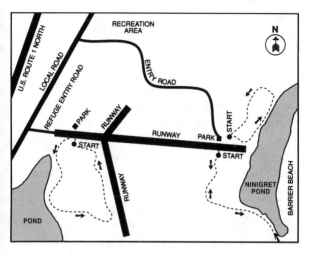

both found by exiting the northbound side of US 1, about midway between Westerly and Wakefield, and going onto a local road. For the first loop walk near Foster Cove, watch for refuge signs on a marked exit off this side road. This exit leads to a parking area at the west end of an old runway.

Two trails can be walked in Ninigret for a pleasant half-day outing. One is the mentioned simple loop at the west end of the refuge near US 1. The other meanders out to a point of land with fine views over Ninigret Pond, a tidal lagoon. Walks on nearby Ninigret Beach lie close by. Birders will find much of interest here, too, for the protected bodies of water around the refuge host a variety of local and migratory avian species.

A display describing the refuge marks the trailhead. Follow an old woods road south and west from the display board. Red maples and trooping bittersweet vines line the grassy way. You shortly pull around to the southeast in stands of black birch and oak. A boggy slump is passed on the left as the road dips among spotted alders. Although the cover is very dense, occasional views of Foster Cove open to the right as you walk. The grassy road gradually broadens as you turn again to the southwest and, leaving more thickly grown bittersweet and bayberry, come to open views of the cove. This cove, one of several in Ninigret Pond, provides a sheltered, nutrient-rich, tidal resting place and feeding ground for many species of ducks and wading birds.

Pulling away from the water, the path turns east and approaches an old runway. Just before you reach the pavement, the grassy road goes left and north beside a rusted aviation marker that reads STA 6. Walking north, you stay close to the runway, moving past eastern red cedars, black oak, and frequent clusters of alders. Cottontail rabbits seem to find this type of cover desirable habitat and hop about, crossing the path. You are likely to see some of the long ears along the trail as well as red fox. The route pulls west soon amid stands of brilliant goldenrod and staghorn sumac. After a few minutes' walk northwest and west in more cedar growth, you come out onto paved surface just east of the parking area, having completed the loop.

Hop in your car and drive *northeast* a short distance along the same local access road parallel to US 1. Turn *right* into the Ninigret Recreation Area, passing facilities operated by the town of Charlestown, and continue on a paved road that winds between some of the recycled buildings of the old navy base. Continue *eastward* on this paved way, which will bring you to a parking area at another runway site. From here it's just a short walk southeast to another trailhead signboard.

You now have your choice of two trails, both of

which are worth doing in good weather. If you walk east, a short loop trail drops down to the edge of Ninigret Pond. The pond is actually tidal, fed from the open Atlantic through the Charlestown Breachway northward along Ninigret Beach. The east side of the pond is a barrier beach of dunes and white sand that protects this tranquil body of water from the fractious open Atlantic. Birds like it here. Herons, cormorants, and many duck species spend time on these waters. On a recent visit, a beautiful mature swan patrolled the pond and drifted to shore to see if we had anything to offer. This trail follows the edge of the pond northward, then circles around and comes back to the signboard.

The other trail runs south through tall grass and scrub to a junction, where you bear left and approach the pond farther down. Good places for observing avian wildlife lie along here. The path soon crosses an isthmus and continues out to a headland with good outlooks up and down the pond and east to the beach. It is also possible to walk out to the barrier beach from here, adding to the distance you can walk. Return to your car when ready by retracing your steps northward.

You'll find Ninigret most appealing to visit in winter, spring, and autumn, when the insects that thrive in the marshes aren't present. October holds great appeal here for those who like to watch bird migrations. Large populations of migrating coastal birds use Ninigret as a stopping place. For information on the refuge, call (401) 364-9124.

9 · Burlingame State Park

Location: Charlestown, Rhode Island
Distance: 7¾ miles
Walking time: 3½ hours

Watchaug Pond at Burlingame State Park in Charlestown is the focal point for a lengthy, interesting hike that wanders through boardwalked swamps, mixed-growth forestland, and along an attractive shore. This is one of two walks in this book (the other is in Massachusetts) that follows the shoreline of a pond for its full circuit. The nearly 8-mile loop walk around Watchaug will test your mettle as it tucks in and out of the waterside and runs over mostly level ground while circling the 940-acre pond. The route crosses a swamp, takes to both tote and paved roads briefly, and keeps in sight of water a good deal of the way. You could walk parts of the loop and retrace your steps for a shorter hike, but dedicated walkers will commit to the three to four pleasant hours this extended loop requires from start to finish.

Burlingame State Park lies on the inland side of US 1 in West Charlestown. Six miles *south* of the junction of US 1 and RI 110 in Perryville, turn *west* onto well-marked King's Factory Road. Follow this road for just under a mile, watching for a paved lane known as Prosser Trail, which departs at a sharp angle to the *left* and south. Turn down Prosser Trail and enter a large picnic area on your right 0.5 mile below the turn just made. You drop down to a large parking lot on the shores of Watchaug Pond. Keeping *left* across this lot, follow a narrow, bumpy road along the shore for 0.75 mile to Kimball Wildlife Refuge, owned and operated by Rhode Island Audubon. There is room to park in a clearing just beyond the education center. A number of interesting events are scheduled at this center seasonally. Contact Rhode Island Audubon at (401) 231-6444 for information. If you're lucky, you may be able to combine a walk around Burlingame with a program at Kimball Refuge.

To begin, walk back down the road from the Kimball Refuge parking area and look for a white-blazed trail that slips off into the woods to your left within 100 yards of where you parked. The trail drops off the bend in the road and moves over level ground, staying quite close to the pond. Leaving the refuge woodlands, the path shortly enters the Burlingame camping area to the west, crosses a field, and resumes at a blazed rock next to the camp store telephones. You next cross a drive and follow the white blazes along a paved road through the center of the campground. (You should be moving generally west and northwest here. Don't get off the trail by going down any of the various side roads in the campground.) The pavement stops by an outhouse, but you continue westward into the woods on a grassy tote road.

The stately pines of the campground yield to mixed growth as you enter some low terrain and cross an outlet brook. The white blazes you've been watching for as you walk are now suddenly blue, but stay on this trail a bit longer. The N/S markers that also appear in this sec-

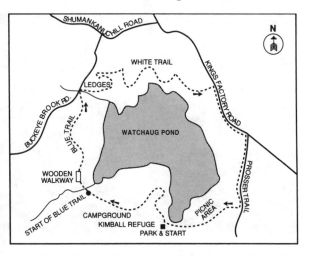

tion refer to the North-South Trail, a statewide long-distance trail presently under construction. Soon the tote road pulls left and you continue straight on, arriving momentarily at a boardwalk that carries you, high and dry, over a swamp at Watchaug's southwest corner. The swamp presses in on either side, dense alder and maple scrub as far as the eye can see.

Beyond this lowland, you proceed northward next on another tote road for about ½ mile, and then go left through a corridor of trees and scrub, coming out on paved Buckeye Brook Road. Walk north on the road a short way, cross a brook, and then carefully pick up the trail again as it reenters the woods to the right. Walking eastward for a moment, you skirt the bottom of some ledges where views back toward the pond are had if you scramble up cautiously. The path now meanders through several esses marked by tree-mounted arrows.

You shortly intersect the white-blazed trail again, turning right and east some distance above the pond's

north shore. (There are occasional views to the pond along here after the autumn leaves have fallen.) You cross a gravel road and proceed through groves of blighted white pines. In moments the white blazes pull sharply to the right. Don't miss this turn. The route now meanders around more ledges, follows a grassy, grown-up road briefly, and then enters a hemlock grove. This is one of those limited spots on this loop where a strong concentration of coniferous trees dominates. Off the trail to the left on a little side trail is a large example of *Ilex opaca*, or American holly.

Continuing eastward, the trail passes several clumps of boulders and some low stone walls. In another ¼ mile you arrive at King's Factory Road. You must now walk about ½ mile rightward and east along the road to its junction with Prosser Trail in order to avoid some private housing along the pond's northeast border. Once at Prosser Trail, follow it to the right and eventually down to the picnic area passed earlier. You may wish to stop here to eat your lunch before walking the final distance to where you left your car. There are opportunities to get to the water's edge in a number of spots on this final leg of the hike.

The circuit around Watchaug Pond is a robust, challenging one at any time of year and is usually most attractive in spring and autumn, when the woods are either greening out or ablaze with color. In October and November it is wise to check with Rhode Island Fish and Wildlife before walking, as some parts of Burlingame are open to hunting in-season.

10 · Trustom Pond
National Wildlife Refuge

Location: South Kingstown, Rhode Island
Distance: 2 miles
Walking time: 1½ hours

The 160 acres of Trustom Pond occupy the center of the rolling, 600-acre Alfred Morse Homestead, a national wildlife refuge since it was taken over by the U.S. Fish and Wildlife Service in 1974. A hidden southern New England gem, Trustom Pond is itself a protected coastal impound divided from the open Atlantic by a substantial barrier beach. Walkers here enjoy a series of attractive, graded trails that wind through open pastures, along quiet shoreline, and among clusters of dense woodland. The paths transit level ground, and the walking is easy for hikers of all abilities. Given its location, this route is of special interest to bird-watchers, too.

An important link in the Atlantic Flyway, Trustom Pond provides a safe nesting and refueling place for literally thousands of migratory birds. Resident bird populations are also substantial. Red-tailed hawks, ospreys, marsh hawks (northern harriers), orioles, catbirds, field sparrows, red-winged blackbirds, and others have long seasons at Trustom. A number of aquatic birds, includ-

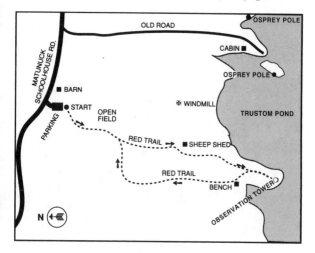

ing various species of ducks and waders, will also be seen in the refuge. A comprehensive birding guide, such as the *National Audubon Field Guide to North American Birds: Eastern Region* or the Peterson guides, should be in your jacket pocket when you walk here, and binoculars are essential. Because so many birds are visible at Trustom except in the dead of winter, you will do well to walk quietly, the better to get within binocular range. This isn't an appropriate walk for noisy groups, and dogs are banned to spare bird and animal life from harassment.

The Trustom Pond Refuge lies just off US 1 in South Kingstown and *east* of Charlestown. Watch for Moonstone Beach Road on the ocean side of US 1 and follow it a mile generally *southward* to Matunuck Schoolhouse Road. Bear *right* and follow Matunuck Road about 0.75 mile to the well-marked entrance to the refuge on the *left.* Park your car in the lot near the trailhead.

Walk the gravel feeder trail southwest out of the

parking area to reach the larger trail network. The path runs through some tangled scrub, common greenbrier and jack pine, arriving in minutes at an open pasture. The trail forms a T here, and you bear right then immediately left, walking south through a column of trees that serves as a windbreak and provides a source of berries to small birds. The trail moves straight down the pasture, where bobolinks, field sparrows, robins, warblers, meadowlarks, and other small birds nest in the grass or in the bordering scrub.

Reaching a stone wall, you go straight ahead through the opening and into a second field, once pasture but now reverting to brush. A couple of solitary jack pines stand in the middle of the field, surrounded by great clumps of goldenrod. Narrow deer paths emerge from the thicket that lies to the left, crossing the field and reentering the woods to the west. Cottontail rabbits enjoy nibbling on the grasses here.

At the end of this second field your southward march

gets interrupted for a moment, as you go right and west at the low end of the field. A short uphill walk brings you to another trail junction in the woods where, by some pines, you bear left and south again on a broad path toward the pond. The path makes a shady passage through dense woods where red maples, spotted alder, red oak, and a variety of woodferns flourish. A stone wall follows the path for a distance. Now you are close enough to the pond to hear some of the waterbirds that frequent these waters.

A junction is reached soon, and you bear left, walking over a series of hummocks, where occasional openings permit views of the pond eastward. In autumn the distinct, plaintive honking of large flocks of Canada geese can be heard here, and often they can be seen if you approach quietly. The path now heads along a narrow spit of land, with the pond on both sides. In spring and autumn particularly, the silent hiker will have a chance to observe the many varieties of ducks, waders, and geese that crowd the pond. Benches are situated at the end of the neck where the trail ends. Here some of the resident mute swans of Trustom Pond may be seen, as may ospreys (fish hawks) and green and great blue herons. The barrier beach can be seen over to the south. With lunch in the pack and binoculars in hand, you can rest here contentedly, observing a tremendous amount of bird activity, hearing the ocean crashing in the distance, light to the ear. On a sunny April or October day, you'll be in no hurry to leave.

When the spirit moves, retrace your steps off the neck and back to the last trail junction. Go left, northwest and north now, as the trail winds along a dense alder swamp, making its way steadily toward the road. A trail is passed on the right, but you continue northward, then bear east and right about ½ mile above the pond. A short walk uphill eastward brings you back to the stone wall dividing the two pastures walked through earlier. At the break in the stone wall, turn left, cross the field, and retrace your steps northward to the parking lot.

This walk, as described, is just over 2 miles in length. If you have the time and inclination when back in the upper pasture, you can head east and south on a path that eventually runs over an old road to another point of land where the small, seasonal osprey population can be seen at close range. Allow an hour and a half more to complete this additional leg, which merits your time if you desire some further exercise.

II · Great Swamp Management Area

Location: West Kingston, Rhode Island
Distance: 5 miles
Walking time: 2½ hours

A wild, densely wooded place, the 3,000-acre Great Swamp Management Area provides interesting, secluded tramping in south coastal Rhode Island below Kingston. This enormous lowland is managed as a game area and is home to muskrat, raccoon, and deer. A range of woodland nesting birds and aquatic species rest here. Big trees and power-line poles around the central marsh also contain the nests of a small, resurgent population of ospreys or fish hawks, as they are sometimes called. Several trails that proceed along old woods roads find their way through Great Swamp, and the walking is mostly level and undemanding. It's possible to put together a loop walk of 3 to 5 miles on dry ground here while circling a watery impoundment just east of the Usquopaug River. Because of its low, marshy character, the management area may be buggy in high summer. Late winter and spring favor the hiker at Great Swamp. Fall walking is also possible, but some sections of the preserve are open to hunting. For your safety, check with local fish and game officers before walking here during hunting season.

Entry to the Great Swamp lies off US 1, about midway between Providence and New London. Four miles *south* of the US 1-RI 4 junction near LaFayette, go *west* on RI 138. Pass the University of Rhode Island campus and, at a point 6 miles *west* of US 1, watch for Liberty Lane, a side road on your *left*. Liberty Lane goes *west* nearly a mile until the pavement runs out alongside railroad tracks. The road, now dirt, follows the tracks southwest and south into the preserve. Pass the first set of headquarters buildings and continue south to a blocked side road on the left, where parking is available. On the local park map this is known as Area I.

The walk begins at this turnout and goes south on the main gravel road, which bends through dense deciduous woods where blueberries, huckleberries, and blackberries abound. Black alder and red maple closely border the road as a junction is reached. Keep left at the junction, passing a range of dead trees on the left and a grove of rare American holly on the right. The holly, leafed in brilliant, waxy green, is an unlikely resident this far north, though it flourishes in a few protected pockets here and in coastal southern Massachusetts.

Walking under a power line in the open, you reenter the woods where common greenbrier grows plentifully around swamp maples and black cherry trees. Club mosses and a profusion of ferns line the path. The trail rises slightly past open pasture, kept clear to support upland game. A trail is passed on the right and another, shortly, on the left. Continue south and southwest on the gravel road, coming in a few minutes to an area dotted with boulders and humps of exposed ledge. Beyond the boulder field you arrive at the shore of Worden Pond, the site of a seaplane hangar and a preferred

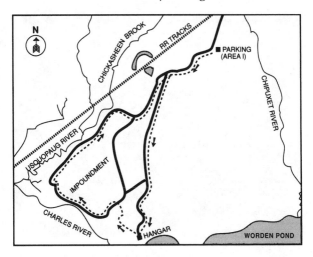

hangout for fishermen. Here you are at the southern-
most extent of the walk, not quite 2 miles from your
starting point. You may want to rest here for a while,
enjoying views out over the 1,000-acre catchment of
tranquil Worden Pond.

The route next runs west and northwest from back of
the hangar on a wet, swampy path that rises to higher
ground quickly. Walking by several open fields, you pass
a road on the right and continue north (and left) until
you emerge on another graded dirt road. Bear left on
the dirt road and walk down to a dike that holds back
the considerable impounded waters of a network of
small streams. Water lilies, cattail, and sweet gale grow
thickly along the border. Kingfishers perch above the
water, making diving raids on small fish. Great blue and
green herons wade the shallows, and Canada geese stop
here, too.

If you proceed northwest along the dike, the power
lines seen earlier again come into view. Here you are

likely to see ospreys in spring and summer. These fish hawks have built large nests of marsh grass, big sticks, and twigs in trees or on the power-line poles that trail off northward. A catwalk runs out into the impoundment and makes a good observation platform for viewing local avian wildlife. Use caution if you go out on the catwalk, especially in wet weather. At no time should the nests be approached.

The path continues around the impoundment, pulling gradually to the north by clumps of maple and some dead, drowned trees. You move away from final views of the water. Climbing, you reenter mixed-growth woods, go briefly under the power line, and work your way eastward a short distance until you reach the dirt access road once again. Go left and north on this road, passing what is known as Management Area II on the left as you proceed to the parking area where you began this walk.

The entire loop, from roadhead to Worden Pond,

around the marsh, and back to the parking lot, is about 5 miles in length. It can be walked in a brisk two hours. But, allowing time for exploration of the shores along Worden Pond and some attention to osprey and other bird activity along the impoundment, three to four hours is a more realistic time for completing the Great Swamp circuit. Although most of the hike runs over dry gravel, there are some wet spots, so use waterproof footwear. Binoculars, water, and a lunch belong in your day pack, too.

The Great Swamp supports a significant game population and attracts hunters by the carload in autumn. As mentioned earlier, if you plan to hike here in October and November, better consult with Rhode Island Fish and Wildlife to determine the actual dates of deer and, later, waterfowl open seasons. The swamp is best avoided at these times for your safety. Rhode Island Audubon can provide information on the best dates for sighting nesting ospreys.

12 · Norman Bird Sanctuary

Location: Middletown, Rhode Island
Distance: 1 to 4 miles (depending on route selected)
Walking time: 1 to 3 hours

Just back from the Sakonnet River and the Atlantic, and near the national wildlife refuge at Sachuest Point, the Norman Bird Sanctuary in Middletown provides walkers with access to an extensive network of pretty trails in 450 acres of marsh, wooded upland, and rolling fields. Trails skirt several small ponds on either side of Third Beach Road, easily ascend ridges, and circle pastures and swamps in Norman's northern precincts. The gift of Mabel Norman Cerio, the Norman Sanctuary offers nature exhibits and a series of educational programs. Inquire at the headquarters building for information. A number of larger wild birds that have been injured and cannot fly are cared for here also. You'll find literally miles of pleasant walking in the Norman Sanctuary, and can put together a walking route that interests you, or simply take one of the four trips described here.

Trails at Norman Sanctuary rarely seem overvisited, especially on weekdays, and are open to walking seven days a week from nine to five. Guided birding walks are conducted on Sunday morning. Information on edu-

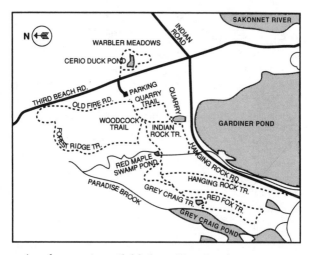

cational events is available by calling (401) 846-2577. A small fee is charged for entry.

To walk in Norman Sanctuary, take RI 138 *east* from Newport center. RI 138 becomes Miantonomi Avenue, which, in turn, becomes Green End Avenue. Once on Green End Avenue proceed eastward, watching for Third Beach Road, where you go *right*. Just a mile down Third Beach Road, turn into the sanctuary parking area on the *right*. A general guide to the Norman Sanctuary and an excellent map of all sanctuary trails are available in the barn where you register.

Before setting out you may wish to visit the wild birds that are housed at the sanctuary. Sanctuary staff provide information to the public on the care of injured or orphaned birds and mammals. A variety of birds, some injured in the wild but most shot or harmed by humans, are sheltered here in room-sized flying cages. On a recent visit I found two splendid red-tailed hawks, a broad-winged hawk, a glowering great horned owl, and a crow in residence. None of these birds could survive in the wild. Natural history exhibits and video programs are also set up in the barn.

Rather than describe a single route to follow, I recommend a number of the paths here. They may be walked individually, or you can link them together as a series of connected routes to be traveled over a long day's hike on a fine weekend. Take along some binoculars, water, and a lunch and lose yourself in the woods here for a day.

A network of interesting trails covers the eastern and northern section of Norman Sanctuary. Register at the barn and try some of the following:

1. Warbler Meadows Trail is a cluster of short interconnected trails across Third Beach Road around diminutive Cerio Duck Pond. This walk covers low, level ground in an area where resident and migratory waterbirds may be seen.

2. The Old Fire Road, Forest Ridge Trail, and Woodcock Trail provide a varied loop through both marsh and woodlands in the northern limits of the park. Black locust, red maple, black cherry, and black gum trees line the paths. To connect with these trails, head north from the junction outside the barn.

3. The Indian Rock Trail and Quarry Trail are short routes that loop through a quartz-rich series of rock ribs, passing through fields and shrubs congenial to such resident wildlife as fox, woodcock, and pheasant. To walk in the western area of the sanctuary near the ponds, take the connector path west to Red Maple Swamp Pond. This pond, though stagnant, is a pretty spot to observe active bird life. A number of

species nest in the dry-ki and forest in or around the pond.

4. The Grey Craig Trail runs west, then south, along the ridges above Grey Craig Pond. The return can be made on the Red Fox Trail. Fine views of Gardiner Pond and the Atlantic are beheld on the geologically interesting Hanging Rock Trail. The 300-million-year-old Narragansett formation rock that forms this ridge (sometimes known as Berkeley's Seat) is a

metamorphosed conglomerate called puddingstone. This walk departs southward from Red Maple Swamp Pond and is probably the premier walk in the sanctuary.

If you live in southern New England, give strong consideration to becoming a member of the Norman Sanctuary. Membership dues guarantee free trail access, discounts in the sanctuary store, and a list of other benefits. Admission fees and membership income support sanctuary operations and other conservation efforts in the Aquidneck region.

13 · Ruecker Wildlife Refuge

Location: Tiverton, Rhode Island
Distance: 2 miles
Walking time: 2 hours

Rhode Island Audubon Society's Ruecker Wildlife Refuge in Tiverton serves up good four-season walking in a riverfront setting in the eastern quarter of the state. Newport-born artist Emilie Ruecker donated this 47-acre refuge in 1965. Today these lands bordering the broad Sakonnet River support a cluster of inviting trails that roam quiet riverfront lowlands not far southwest of Mount Hope Bay. If both walking and birding are among your interests, this pleasant, easy walk through Audubon's Ruecker Refuge offers an interesting half day's diversion.

The refuge is seasonal or year-round home to more than 130 bird species, so bring binoculars and an Audubon or Peterson guide in your day pack when visiting here. The Ruecker Refuge makes a particularly good destination in spring and autumn, before or after the considerable local mosquito population rises from the marshes and asserts its rights. Winter walking can be done here, too, though with the trees barren of leaves the refuge is less shielded from nearby farms and houses. If you come in summer, bring insect repellent.

Ruecker Refuge lies along the eastern perimeter of

Rhode Island, just south of Tiverton and north of the point where the Sakonnet widens to become a bay. The refuge can be reached easily from Providence (via I-95) or Boston (I-93). In either case, follow RI 24 *southwest* from Fall River to RI 77 at Tiverton. Turn onto RI 77, drive exactly 3.5 miles *southward*, and bear *right* at Seapowet Avenue. You'll find the refuge parking area 0.25 mile in on the *right*.

This route will take you through all three areas of Ruecker Refuge. We begin by walking the Red Trail, which runs northeast from the parking area. You pass a copse of apple trees, remnants of the farm once located here. Red maples grow along the trail, and you are soon in a cedar and hickory thicket. In a few more steps you cross the Orange Trail (a tractor road) and reenter the woods. Bur oaks grow above ledges of puddingstone, a sedimentary rock of the Narragansett Basin. The path continues north through beech and oak. Common greenbrier, viburnum, and honeysuckle grow in dense thickets here. More eastern red cedars are seen as the trail pulls away from the refuge boundary, crosses a stone wall by some big maples, and then goes through the wall once more to emerge on a grassy woods road (the Yellow Trail).

Turn right onto this open path and you come in a few yards to a junction, where you keep right again, walking northwest and then west along the Sakonnet River. Fine views of the river and marshes open up here. The Sakonnet is a tidal river that widens to a bay farther south and connects with Mount Hope Bay to the north. Mount Hope Bay is an arm of Narragansett Bay, so all of these great tidal exchanges are connected. Mussels and fiddler crabs are seen at the shore's edge, and

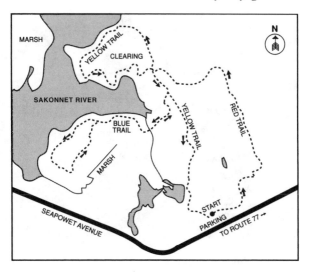

striped bass and bluefish frequent the waters. Saltwort, cordgrass, salt-meadow grass, and sea lavender grow from low to high ground along the banks.

The Yellow Trail works its way around the point of land and, in stands of cedar, pulls eastward with open views of a tidal marsh to your right. Snowy egrets, glossy ibis, great blue and little blue herons, and black-crowned night herons forage in mudflats and waterways of the marsh, according to Rhode Island Audubon. Passing a couple of benches, the trail continues east and returns to the beginning of this northern loop. Proceed south on the Yellow Trail along a stone wall, watching for the Blue Trail on the right.

Take the Blue Trail southwest as it drops through a corridor of black cherry growth and thick woodferns to a shingle path that divides a small pond from the larger marsh and the open river beyond. A footbridge is

crossed, and you then walk northwest along the marshy inlet of the Sakonnet again. In summer months sandpipers, yellowlegs, and plover skitter over and through the marsh. The path follows the shore, looping left to the southwest amid clumps of shadbush and bayberry. If you arrive in spring, the white blossoms of the shadbush are usually the first of the season in the woods.

Gradually the Blue Trail circles the end of the point, running southeast and then northeast in groves of oak. You now head back to the footbridge and up the slight rise to the Yellow Trail, where you bear right and south. The walk next runs in the open on a grassy way, but, as you approach the parking area, remnants of an old apple orchard are found. Dark, old spruce and some scattered pine also border the path, their branches bound with aggressive bittersweet vines. The Audubon guide to the refuge points out that this section is an important one for birds. Titmice, sparrows, chickadees, tree swallows, and eastern phoebes are all sighted, as are vireos, mourning doves, and gray catbirds. Bobwhite and pheasant are also present. Continuing southward, you return to the parking lot shortly.

This circuit around the three zones of the refuge that are accessible to walkers can be easily covered in less than two hours, longer if you pause to monitor bird flight from time to time. A relaxed pace is recommended. Binoculars and waterproof footwear are useful gear for those who wish to explore the marsh at water's edge. If you enjoy your visit to Ruecker, please show your appreciation by lending support to the work of Rhode Island Audubon.

III. Massachusetts

14 · Lowell Holly Reservation

Location: Mashpee, Massachusetts
Distance: 1½ miles
Walking time: 1½ hours

A hammerhead-shaped promontory jutting into the midst of two of the Cape's larger ponds, the Lowell Holly Reservation is owned by the Trustees of Reservations in Massachusetts. The reservation takes its name from a former owner, Abbott Lawrence Lowell, president of Harvard University from 1909 to 1933. President Lowell made a gift of these exceptional 130 acres for public use in 1943. The notable American holly trees, *Ilex opaca*, which are a key focus of the reservation, are well distributed throughout the grounds, fine specimens of a species at the top of its range (see also Walk 19, Albert Norris Reservation).

Positioned in Mashpee at the head of the long arc of varied terrain that constitutes Cape Cod, Lowell Holly Reservation provides some interesting walking in a setting of considerable attractiveness. Temperate in climate due to its proximity to the ocean both north and south, the reservation shelters some trees and shrubs usually found more to the south in the sandy soil of the immediate coastal plain. A series of well-marked woods roads and paths cross this point of land, and the walker will find anywhere from one to several hours of pleasant exploration here between the ponds. Though officially open May through October, the reserve can be negotiated by the walker almost any time of year.

If you'd like to walk here, travel US 6 for 4 miles *east* of MA 3 and the Sagamore Bridge. Turn right and *south* onto MA 130 at Exit 2. Driving *south,* watch for South Sandwich Road on your *left* about 7.25 miles below US 6. Turn here and just a short distance up this side road to the north, you'll find the gravel entry to the reservation on the *left* where there are several white signs with the names of private residents and the number 186. Head in to the reservation gate, which may be closed if you arrive at any time other than the official summer season. Room to park lies to the left and right of the gate. Please do not venture onto adjacent private property, or block the road. (In-season you can drive in to a parking lot 0.5 mile inside the gate, but then you'd miss a nice section of this walk, and on weekends you'll be charged for the privilege. It's best to leave your car by the gate.)

The hiker's route simply follows the woods road northwestward from the gate through red oaks covered with lichens. A grove of white pines borders the west side of the path. Meandering to the north through a stand of beech, you come upon limited winter views to the west to Mashpee Pond. The first of the American hollies you'll see on this walk is soon passed on the right. Watch for the unmistakable, brilliant shiny green of *Ilex opaca*'s prickly leaves. More beeches, lofty ones, are seen as you continue northward, descending slightly. You pass a bog on the right shortly and arrive soon at a clearing where picnic tables and a designated parking area dominate a narrow neck.

Keeping to the right, go beyond the picnic area to the north on a sometimes muddy woods road that sticks

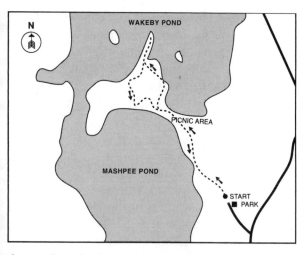

close to the right shore. Boggy stands of alders and other scrub crowd the road to the left. Wakeby Pond lies to the east. Regardless of the temperature inland, it's likely to be cool here on a summer day: The wind rolls across open water from either side of this neck. I've noted a 15- or 20-degree difference in temperature between this spot and the main gate on an otherwise sultry April day.

Very shortly, turn right onto a white-circle-blazed trail that leaves the road by a holly tree and a giant oak. The trail follows the shore due north through stands of red pine, holly, red maple, and great clusters of rhododendrons. These impressive, rangy shrubs grow in thickets inland of the trail. Bright green club moss, the color of sunlight through an empty wine bottle, blankets the pathway.

Descending into a boggy area opposite an island, the trail then quickly surmounts a rise and drops once more. You make an abrupt left turn here and walk west around what seems like at least an acre of rhododendrons.

Going uphill again, the trail marches northwest, arriving at a junction on high ground overlooking Wakeby Pond. The short side trail to the right drops to a sand spit beyond a grove of beeches. Staying on the main trail, you pull around to the southwest. The woods are open and less dense on this north side of the peninsula, and you can gaze across the water to the farther shore.

Another junction comes up soon, and here you can make a detour on what is called the Wheeler Loop, which runs around the west side of the point. That trail goes right and northwest at this junction and rejoins the main trail farther on. Staying on the white-circle-blazed trail, you skirt a low bog on the left. The woods are dark and quiet here, the deadwater trailing off to the southeast. Some brainless wag has carved the legend DAMAGE INC. on a nearby tree.

Turning gradually toward the south, the trail soon meets the return of the Wheeler Loop, which comes in on the right. You pass some openings in the brush to the sandy north shore of Mashpee Pond. On a spring or summer day, fishermen troll the shallows, looking for a strike. The path, now widened to a road, runs uphill and southeast. Downy woodpeckers flit from tree to tree. A solitary Canada goose soars honking over the treetops, bound for the other pond. The trail now comes to its original junction by the big oak. You continue south through the low spot and walk back to the picnic area. Places to swim are found on either side of the neck if you arrive in high summer.

To reach the gate and your car, retrace your steps out the entry road. The entire walk can be done in an hour and a half. Plan an additional half hour if you include the Wheeler Loop in your walk.

15 · Nickerson State Park, Cliff Pond Trail

Location: Brewster, Massachusetts
Distance: 3 miles
Walking time: 2 hours

Eighteen-hundred-acre Nickerson State Park is lodged about mid-Cape, equidistant from the Sagamore Bridge and Provincetown. The park, on the northerly rim of Cape Cod's arc in Brewster, is home to a well-developed network of walking, cycling, and cross-country ski trails that navigate fine coastal woodlands dotted with serene clear-water ponds. The reservation also offers more than four hundred camping spaces for tents and recreational vehicles. Good fishing and swimming in nine bodies of water plus opportunities for canoeing and boating provide further incentive for visiting here. The park makes an excellent destination for day hikers year-round, or, in-season, a place to camp for several days while walking the park trails and then exploring the outer Cape. Winter, spring, and autumn are the real seasons of choice for the walker on Nickerson's trails.

To reach the park, drive *east* on US 6 from MA 3 and the Sagamore Bridge. Leave US 6 and drive *north* on MA 134 east of Barnstable, connecting with MA 6A in East

Dennis, where you turn *right*. Once on MA 6A, head *east* again to the well-marked park entrance in Brewster. Park information, camping registration, and maps can be obtained at the contact station by the main gate. Once inside the park, drive to the boat-launch area between Cliff and Little Cliff Ponds on the east side of the reservation. You can leave your car in a space on the side of the road just above the boat ramps.

The walk we'll take here may be a new kind of experience for many trampers: The Cliff Pond Trail follows this big pond's entire shoreline, making an excellent 3-mile loop that is never out of sight of water. The trail begins near a sign at the northwest corner of the parking area.

Descend northwest to the Cliff Pond shore through groves of pitch pine and white pine. The trail follows the shore, where you'll have excellent views up and down this sizable body of water. Cliff Pond was created by ice deposition during the last ice age. As the great ice sheet that covered New England retreated, stupendous blocks of ice were left behind. When these isolated remnants of the ice sheet later melted over a considerable period of time, enormous depressions were left in the ground, which soon became collecting places for water. Cape Cod now contains several hundred small lakes and ponds that were developed through such glacial activity. Imagine, if you can, one *piece* of ice big enough to create a depression the size of this pond.

Walking north, you slab the hillside as the trail rises and falls above the bright, sandy shore. Rough in some places, the blue-blazed trail is generally easy to follow if you don't stray inland. Some blowdown and small clusters of oaks come up shortly. You reach the first of sev-

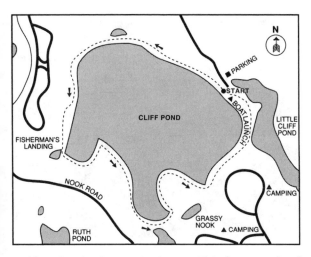

eral beaches in about 15 minutes. This first stretch of
beach belongs to a nearby forestry camp on the hill and
is private property. The trail stays close along the water-
line here and reenters the woods at the end of the beach
in a clump of blowdown. You come to a second beach
in a few more minutes where the trail heads northwest
and west through a grove of pitch pines just in back of
the sand.

The walk along Cliff Pond's north shore takes you
over a narrow lip between the water and a steep hillside covered with young oaks. At a trail junction, stay
left. Fishermen seem to favor this spot, and a number of
Izaak Waltons lounge here, fishing rods propped on
forked sticks at the water's edge. A gully is passed on the
right as you continue west, walking on the beach for a
bit as the trail becomes rough and indistinct. In another ¼ mile you arrive at a sandy area known as Fisherman's Landing, where there is access to the water for
boaters. Stay with the shore as the trail turns south and

then east around the cove, watching for the place where you reenter the woods in some dense scrub.

Once in the woods, the trail runs east toward a point of land, then bears south for some distance along Cliff's west shore. White pine seedlings and spindly oaks grow along the hillside as the trail alternately dips to the shore and then climbs steeply away from the pond. You cross a sandy road and then walk through a depression, working west. A dense grove of white pines lies uphill to the right. Soon you walk more leftward and south on an open woods road at a T. Another junction comes up soon where you cross a sandbar to the left separating Cliff Pond and another body of water known as Grassy Nook.

Your route now runs north along the shore of another point of land where you have good views across the water toward the beaches you walked earlier. The trail gradually pulls east and southeast around the point, the shoreline becoming rockier as you enter another cove.

Continue around the cove, over a rise, and arrive at another sandbar between Cliff and Little Cliff Ponds. The path becomes indistinct here but generally follows the high ground of the bar through some staggered pitch pines and into the woods on the far side. Descend through these woods briefly and emerge at the end of the paved road by the boat ramps. Your car and the trailhead where you began this walk lie just uphill to the north.

This 3-mile circuit around Cliff Pond can be walked steadily in two hours, longer if you stop to rest or swim at some of the cove beaches along the way. Excellent views across the pond exist throughout the entire walk. For other, shorter pond walks at Nickerson, consult the park map.

A note of caution is in order if you're planning to camp here. Nickerson's official camping season runs from April to October (walkers can enter whatever the time of year), but expect few available campsites in late June, July, and August, when seemingly every vacationer in America descends on the Cape. If you wish to camp in high season, make reservations early.

16 • Cape Cod National Seashore, Fort Hill Trail

Location: Eastham, Massachusetts
Distance: 1½ miles
Walking time: 1 hour

Eastham lies well out on Cape Cod on US 6. Rising sharply above the wild, expansive Nauset Marsh in Eastham, Fort Hill and its surrounding fields and woodlands transmit a picture of the Cape in all its various ages: the last ice age, the years of early Indian settlement, the years of colonization, and the 19th-century years of whaling and wealth.

Certainly the interaction of geology and ice are visible here. The hill itself is one of a series of glacially deposited kames, or low hills of glacial rubble, dropped here as the Wisconsin ice sheet withdrew. The imprint of humans over time is discernible as well. The Nauset Indians formerly evolved a sophisticated farming and fishing culture here whose antecedents date back four to five thousand years. Further, Eastham became the site of a major European colonial settlement after 1644, the effect of which changed many of the natural features of the outer Cape forever. As for present-day Fort Hill, visit the Penniman House and see how a 19th-century local-boy-turned-sea-captain-and-whaler established for him-

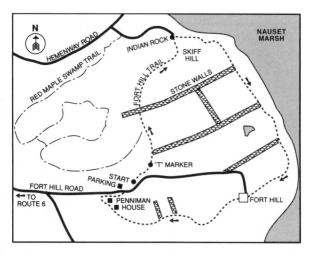

self a country seat high on a hill overlooking the waters
he once navigated.

Driving *northward* toward Provincetown as you
approach the village of Eastham, watch for Governor
Pence Road (also known as Fort Hill Road) on your
right. Turn and follow this road *east* 0.25 mile, passing
the Penniman House, to a parking lot on the *left* just
over the crest of a rise. Arrive here early to assure a spot
for your car if you're walking in high summer or on a
spring or autumn weekend.

A trail that leads through all the representative terrains of the Fort Hill area departs from the far corner
of the parking lot near a Cape Cod National Seashore
map. (For information on other walks in the national
seashore, go to the Salt Pond Visitors Center, just off
US 6 in Eastham center. See also Walks 17 and 18.)
Descend northeast through a slump and into a grove
of black locust trees. You'll see a stone marker with the
initial T on it. This stands for Samuel Treat, a fiery Puri-

tan divine (1648–1717) who preached hellfire and damnation to both whites and Indians in this town for 45 years. The stone marks the corner boundary of land that Treat owned.

Pulling to the left and rising slightly, you come to an open meadow, one of the remnants of local farming activity. (Corn, rye, fruit, and fodder were grown in this area from the time of the early Indian communities onward until as recently as the 1940s.) In a row of red cedars on your left the Red Maple Swamp Trail runs off into a boggy lowland. Pass this trailhead, keeping it in mind in case you want to do additional walking after you complete the Fort Hill Loop.

The trail now goes across the high ground on the west border of the meadow, with splendid views east to the Nauset Marsh and out to the open ocean. Blackberries grow to the left among cedars and black cherry trees. The roar of the waves from the ocean surf nearly a mile away drifts over the fields. In minutes you reenter the woods by a stile as the trail becomes a narrow corridor in more cedar growth. Field sparrows build nests in the thick branches of the cedars; the insistent feeding demands of their newly hatched young are audible in April and May. Little sun enters this dense canopy, and the path remains cool even on warm days.

The trail shortly opens to a clearing on Skiff Hill. Splendid views, northwest to northeast, reward your effort here. A roofed shelter covers some interpretive markers next to Indian Rock, a glacial erratic used by Nauset Indians to sharpen their tools and weapons. Grooves in the rock testify to these activities. The life of the marsh is visible from this spot, too. More than 20 species of aquatic birds reside in or pass through the

marsh during migrations. When Samuel de Champlain visited these waters in 1605, he commented favorably on the Indian settlements around this scene, later naming the place Port de Mallebarre.

Walk southeast next through the woods, soon emerging into the open. Bear left briefly, paralleling an old stone wall, and then go southeast again along the border of the fields just above the shore. Great clusters of Japanese honeysuckle grow rampant on the banking to your left. Ahead to the south you can see Fort Hill. Red-tailed hawks occasionally pause in a solitary apple tree in the field. A second stone wall is passed near the marsh as you begin a short uphill march surrounded by densely growing *Rosa rugosa*. The buzzing chirrup of many red-winged blackbirds can be heard in spring and summer as they stake their territorial claims. The trail bears right and west around another glacial erratic and rises through a black cherry copse to the top of little Fort Hill.

Try to ignore the unnecessary building of a road to the top of this otherwise pristine hill. The unfortunate coming and going of cars piloted by confused tourists who have lost the ability to walk shouldn't be allowed to interfere with your enjoyment of the striking 360-degree views from the hilltop. You can visually take in about a 5-mile stretch of the outer Cape from this point. From here, head downhill and westward across the pasture and into dense woods once more. More black locusts flourish in this cool, moist lowland. The trail passes the ruins of a stone wall and a cattail bog. Walking through more of the prolific red cedars, you rise to the grounds of the Captain Edward Penniman House.

This fine old French Empire–style house was built in 1868 by Captain Penniman, a former harpooner, chief officer of a whaling bark, and seven times circumnavigator of the watery parts of the globe. Born in Eastham in 1831, Penniman retired here in 1884, having taken care to give himself a view of his orchards, fields, and the sea from a cupola on top of the house. When you have looked over the well-preserved manse, it's only a short diagonal walk east across the road to the place where you left your car earlier.

If you wish to explore further, make the loop around the Red Maple Swamp Trail to Skiff Hill, returning south on the Fort Hill Trail across the top of the meadow. The main walk described can be done in an hour. Add another half hour if you decide to complete the swamp loop also.

17 · Cape Cod National Seashore, Nauset Marsh Trail

Location: Eastham, Massachusetts
Distance: 1 mile
Walking time: 1 hour

The New England littoral is not what it once was—nor, for that matter, is Cape Cod. The lengthy curve of the Cape, instantly recognizable on a map, is actually the high ground of a more extensive coastal shelf that was submerged under a 2-mile-thick ice sheet roughly twenty-one thousand to eleven thousand years ago. This weighty, massive ice formation depressed much of the New England coast, ground down higher elevations, and then raised the ocean's depth by several hundred feet as the ice slowly melted. Today's Cape and the major offshore islands are what remains of the high ridges or peaks, liberally covered with glacial till dropped as the ice receded.

As you visit or walk in this region, you are proceeding atop the remains of this formerly greater landmass that depression, scouring, subsequent weathering, erosion, harvesting, and grazing have reduced to the narrow, sandy spit of terrain we know today. In different ways, various sections of the northeastern coast show

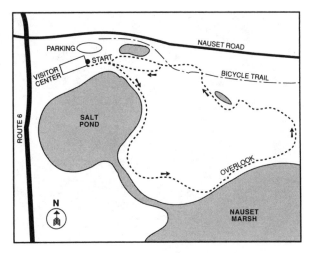

the effects of this stupendous glacial transformation. The granitic hills of Maine's Mount Desert Island, for example, display grooving across their uppermost surfaces as testament to glacial abrasion. Cape Cod's numerous kettle holes, caused by the imprint of enormous, slow-melting blocks of fractured glacial ice, verify prior glacial activity.

On the Nauset Marsh Trail you see a saltwater kettle pond and other interesting evidence of both natural and human intervention in the shaping of this coastal landscape. The Nauset Marsh Trail walk can, ideally, be combined with Walk 16, Fort Hill, also in Eastham. The two together provide an excellent firsthand experience of glaciated coastal landforms and their subsequent human transformation.

To walk this route, travel *east* on US 6 to the town of Eastham on outer Cape Cod. Go to the National Seashore Visitor Center at the corner of US 6 and Nauset Road in Eastham. Leave your car in the center's lot, pos-

sibly visiting some of the center's displays and the rather good regional bookshop inside. The center also schedules tours, lectures, and demonstrations on coastal ecology.

The Nauset Marsh Trail begins by the outdoor amphitheater, behind and below the visitors center. The trail drops quickly east and southeast through a red cedar wood to the shore of Salt Pond. Before you, usually thronged with ducks and other seabirds, lies a perfect example of a saltwater kettle pond. Formerly a freshwater pond, it is now fed by a narrow waterway connecting it with the marsh and, eventually, the open ocean. Tidal infusions bring with them a variety of marine organisms. Like many intertidal bodies of water, this one accepts both salt water from the marsh and freshwater runoff from surrounding uplands.

Walking around the left shore of the pond, its banking grown up with black oak, cedar, and other scrub, you come to the point where the pond tapers to the channel. Go over a little rise here and then out onto an arm of the marsh. Here you walk over a dike and a small wooden footbridge. Views to the east and southeast are of the large marsh to seaward. Shortly, you enter the woods by a stile and climb briskly through a series of curves in closely grown red cedar, black oak, honeysuckle, and pitch pine. The walk, on higher ground now, continues northeastward to a fine overlook above the marsh. The views here are extraordinary: You can spy all of the back marsh and much of the barrier beach (Nauset Spit) that protects it from the direct effects of the aggressive open ocean. In precolonial times most of this marsh was open, navigable water. Over a period of several hundred years, tidal deposition of sediment carried by alongshore currents filled in the protected bay. As the national seashore trail brochure remarks: "Typical of salt marshes, the area is a full-scale nursery for oceanic fish, shellfish and microscopic plankton. It also serves as an important habitat along the Atlantic flyways for shorebirds, wading birds and waterfowl."

The trail descends to the marsh floor and then climbs north and northwest through more dense cedar. This seeming primeval wood is actually quite recent. The ground you walk here was a private golf course until about 60 years ago, believe it or not. Left to its own devices, nature has quickly reasserted itself. The trail now descends southwestward, skirting a stagnant pond where peepers loudly serenade would-be mates in spring and summer. Emerging from the woods, you cross a paved bicycle trail twice, working your way westward. In minutes, after passing through a stand of locusts, you arrive at a junction with the Button Bush Trail, at which you keep left.

This short loop trail is a self-guiding walk for the blind and handicapped. The path has a guide rope and trail markers in Braille along its length. Three cheers for this excellent idea that makes it possible for *everyone* to enjoy a woods walk.

Continuing westward past Norway spruce, black oak, and cherry, you head in the direction of the visitors center. A female cardinal flits from branch to branch. In the thick scrub to the left of the trail are beach plum and bayberry. Walking into the sunset, you arrive in a few more yards at your starting point.

The walk around Salt Pond and Nauset Marsh takes about an hour. If you walk here in the middle of summer, insect repellent may be necessary for comfort.

18 · Cape Cod National Seashore, The Provincelands

Location: Provincetown, Massachusetts
Distance: 1 mile
Walking time: 1¼ hours

Like a kind of geological cake, more than 90 percent of Cape Cod rests on an underlayment of glaciated, exposed upland frosted with glacial till. But at the Cape's outermost tip, the walker finds less subtantial stuff. The land around present-day Provincetown did not exist when the rest of the Cape underwent its most recent glaciation, beginning approximately twenty-one thousand years ago. In fact, the tip of Cape Cod is almost brand new when compared geologically with the other four-fifths of its length from Truro westward.

At its outer extremity, the Provincelands constitute a unique chunk of this Cape Cod landscape. Probably about five thousand years old, the Provincelands consist of sand and gravel plucked from the older section of the Cape. These materials were carried by shore currents and shaped by wind action into rolling dunes. Subsequent wind action and weathering created sand spits, enclosed pools, and, later, the basis for vegetation. Put more simply, the very existence of the Provincelands is due to an accident of erosion and prevailing winds. For the same reasons, much of this terrain remains unstable today.

To walk the Provincelands, drive to the Beech Forest trailhead via US 6 to the outskirts of Provincetown. Just before you reach the built-up area, go *right* or *north* at the lights onto Race Point Road. Watch now for a marked entrance on the *left* and park in the Provincelands lot. The trail leaves from the northeast corner of the parking area.

According to the *Beech Forest Trail Guide*, which is available at the trailhead, the Provincelands appear to have been densely forested when the Pilgrims made landfall here in 1620. Within a hundred years overcutting of timber, forest fires, and overgrazing had reduced the area to an amorphous, sandy landmass of shifting dunes. In fact, this sandy substrate became so mobile that a number of families were forced to move their houses away on sledges rather than see them buried by drifting sand. Sadly, ecological destruction seems to have been an accepted part of American life from the earliest days of settlement. Even then, however, there were those in the population who recognized the folly of denuding the earth, and a slow process of implementing controls throughout the 1800s and early 1900s brought reforestation. The beech forest you will walk through at the Provincelands represents a rare living reminder of the mixed-growth forest probably characteristic of presettlement days on the outer Cape.

Begin by entering the woods in a northeasterly direction on the Pond Loop, walking through some young aspens and oaks and coming immediately to a wooden bridge where you have good views over the lower pond. This trail actually cuts a long oval through the

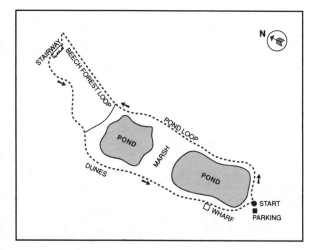

woods, skirting two dunes and two small, sunken ponds. Continue northwestward over a boardwalk and along the east shore of the pond. Wild blueberry, beach plum, and bayberry flourish here along the banking. Black locust and more oak grow randomly along the path. As you proceed, the trail becomes more sandy. Whatever ground cover lies here is very thin. Underneath, all is sand, as becomes very clear shortly when, rounding a bend, the shoulder of a dune becomes visible. You have a brief uphill climb now under pitch pines on a trail that has become, for the moment, buried in drifting sand. The great dune to the right meanders eastward, its substance slowly migrating to the west across the path. In this spot you can see for yourself the fragility and instability of this terrain.

The route next follows the shore of a second, smaller pond. Sarsaparilla, highbush blueberries, and several young beeches are passed. A carpet of club moss covers some of the trail. Tupelo black gum trees and catbrier

grow near the water's edge. You catch glimpses of the pond to the left, thickly grown up with pondweed, the shore dense with bayberry and, here and there, lush clumps of poison ivy. You arrive next at a trail junction by some birches, where you keep right or north on a boardwalk that leads into a gully. You enter the beech forest, tall gray trunks rising on each side interspersed with the occasional pitch pine higher up on the banking. Here we have the typical upland climax forest we expect to find elsewhere in New England, but which has mostly disappeared on the tip of the Cape through human carelessness. In fall and winter the beeches hold their leaves, and these rattle in the wind like small, folded sheets of papyrus.

The trail abruptly halts in this little grove and now turns and clambers up the steep westerly hillside. From this height-of-land you drop immediately west into another gully, where a second dune looms in front of you. The trail now runs south, paralleling the great arm of sand above and to the right. (Please resist the temptation to climb over the open dunes, even if you can see that others have done so. Human footsteps drastically hasten erosion.)

After walking farther southward over a path defined by log borders, you come again to a trail junction. Keep right and south here, walking well above the two ponds. You can see them better from this side during the walk south. The upper pond is the more obscure, its waters pocked with little islets of dense vegetation. A border of thick scrub divides the two ponds. The acoustics over the lower pond are such that a conversation way down on its south shore can sometimes be heard up here on the dune slope. Either of these small bodies of water may once have been inlets of the sea, but were gradually closed off by sand migration and are slowly becoming freshwater ponds, fed by a shallow water table and runoff.

Descend the sandy trail south and southeast under pitch pines as the route gradually widens. Another pond is seen to the right while you pass swamp azalea, blueberry, checkerberry, and other low shrubs. A few minutes farther on you cross a boardwalk and soon emerge on the northwest side of the lot where you parked.

The walk around the Beech Forest Trail and back adds up to a mile in length and can be done in an hour and a quarter at a leisurely pace. Because the ground is sandy and traction sometimes poor, wear lug-soled heavy shoes or low boots for comfortable walking on this outing.

19 · Albert Norris Reservation

Location: Norwell, Massachusetts
Distance: 1¼ miles
Walking time: 1 hour

A brief drive from Boston, the 100-acre Norris Reservation in Norwell offers an easily walked circuit trail through shady, pleasant woods. The path slabs the quiet shore of the scenic North River as it winds toward the sea. Although this land is near settled areas and houses are not far off, it still provides a feeling of rural remoteness surprising for a reserve so near a town center. On a warm spring day, when the ponds are full and the brooks running full tilt, an unhurried tramp through the Norris Reservation is an excellent means of getting away from the urban rush.

Walkers visiting the Norris Reservation, whether approaching from the north or south, should drive MA 3 to the point where it is crossed by MA 53 on the Norwell-Hanover line. Follow MA 53 less than 0.25 mile *northwest* from its intersection with MA 3, watching for MA 123 on the *right*. Bear *right* on MA 123 (known as Main Street in Norwell) and go *eastward* through Norwell center, watching for Dover Street on the *right* just past the post office. (Dover Street departs Main Street at a sharp angle and is easy to miss if you drive too fast. Look for Dover Street about 3.5 miles from the point where you left MA 3.) After you have turned onto Dover, watch for the Norris Reservation sign and parking area to the immediate *left*. Leave your car here.

The path follows an open cinder road southeastward on level grades. Young white pines and red or pin oaks line the path. In just a few moments you arrive at the site of a pretty, old milldam and pond. A working mill was located on this site as early as 1690. Two watercourses, both channels of Second Herring Brook, are crossed here, the first on a new wooden bridge and the second as it flows through the old millrace. The wreckage of the mill's gear-drive system sticks up out of the water.

Once past the pond, the trail now bears sharply around to the south as you turn right around an old stone wall and walk through a lofty grove of red cedar and white pine. The trail shortly passes through a clearing with a granite outcrop to the left and a disused stone grinding wheel, perhaps from the old mill site, plunked down in the grass. Past the clearing, the trail dips quickly into a dry hollow and then reaches a Y-junction. The brook cuts through the trees to your right.

Walk left and uphill to the east from the trail junction. You're headed for the North River marshes this way. Pines and an occasional beech shelter the quiet, shady right-of-way. This is a cool place to walk on a hot day. You descend through a slump, shortly paralleling a stone wall on your right. The trail next makes a sharp bend right and south where the wall turns a similar corner by a clutch of young maples. Just to the right of and behind the maples is the first of many American holly trees you will see scattered along the route. The brilliant, spiked, shiny green leaves stand out against the less

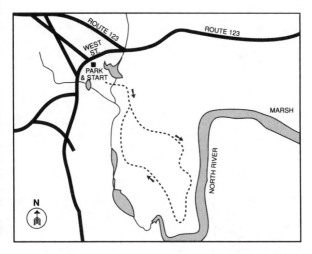

spectacular pines that surround them. The holly is a distinctly southern coastal New England tree. The walker is not likely to see it much farther north than this point, nor far inland.

A series of dead pines and red cedar is passed as the North River comes into view on the left. A side trail departs left, but stay on the main trail, which pulls right and briskly uphill. A little climb is made to the southwest on a hill dotted with more holly. The path now turns south and to the left, meandering downhill through red spruce and scrub along a stone wall. River views open up across the marsh as you descend. You'll walk through three stone walls as you approach the river's edge, soon arriving in a grove of beeches. Two unmarked paths leave the trail and run out onto the marsh in this section. Splendid views up and down the North River are before you, though the marsh may be seasonally wet and rough for walking at times.

Stepping a little farther west, you skirt the edge of the

marsh, with more views south and southeast toward the ocean several miles distant. The marsh is broad and open, and even on mild days you may encounter a stiff wind coming up the river. Putting the water views behind you, walk northwest through still another stone wall and past a marshy area screened by bushes to your left. The trail soon widens to a road. A hillside speckled with oak and holly is passed to the right, where heaps of acorns cover the path. A wall is crossed now, and a sunken bog lies off to the left. The trail rises slightly to a grove of beeches, pulls westward a bit, and comes to a side trail to the left. This path goes to a small pond on private property. Please stay on the main trail here, respecting reservation boundaries.

The route now runs northward through some majestic groves of very old white pines. Another stone wall is crossed. These walls are reminders that this land once saw use as farm smallholdings or pasturage, probably no later than the early 1900s, judging from the size and height of the trees that have taken over. A pine, shattered, split, and stripped by lightning, stands to the left of the trail. In minutes you come to the Y where you turned toward the river earlier. Continue straight ahead and north here, walking uphill to the clearing and then around the milldam site again. Going northwestward, you arrive back at the parking area a few minutes farther on.

The entire loop around the reservation can be walked in an hour at a leisurely pace. Benches have been placed along the trail for those who wish to rest and enjoy the quiet of the woods. Visitors are reminded that cutting any trees or shrubs or starting fires is illegal. The reservation is open year-round. Walkers will find spring and autumn the best months to visit the Norris Reservation. Those arriving in high summer should pack along insect repellent.

20 · World's End Reservation

Location: Hingham, Massachusetts
Distance: 2 miles
Walking time: 2 hours

World's End is the kind of haven that should exist near every major city: a place of natural beauty, separate from the congested world of everyday affairs, a wooded corner of the world to spend an afternoon enjoying the breezes off a harbor and the sound of birdsong. Formed by two low glacial hills (drumlins) connected by a narrow, sandy neck, World's End Reservation is an excellent high ground from which to escape the heat of sweltering days in high summer. In winter the sere beauty of the tree-bordered paths over bare hills is no less inviting as you walk this dramatic peninsula jutting out into Hingham Harbor.

In the late 1800s World's End was owned by John R. Brewer, a leading 19th-century Boston business figure. In 1890 Brewer hired Frederick Law Olmsted, founder of the landscape architecture movement in America, to lay out roads for a resort community in what is now the reservation. Olmsted planned to line his gravel ways with carefully selected trees, placed for maximum aesthetic advantage. Luckily, a proposed 150-home development never got under way, and the peninsula became farmland and, later, a park.

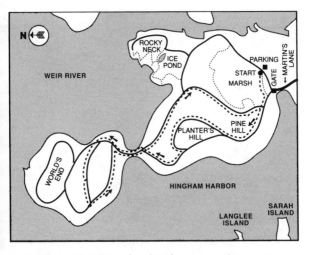

In the mid-1960s the developers again got starry-eyed at the thought of building all over World's End, hoping to plow under this unique landscape, formerly known as Cushing's Neck. A massive effort by concerned residents of Hingham and surrounding towns raised nearly half a million dollars, making it possible for the Trustees of Reservations in Massachusetts to buy the land and protect it forever.

John R. Brewer had begun planting many of the trees Olmsted had specified in the original layout; his heir, Helen Brewer Walker, and her husband, William H. Walker, saw to the continuing protection and maintenance of the park until it came into the Trustees' hands. World's End is today a great monument to private-citizen effort to protect valuable lands. The reservation testifies that, where the conservation ethic is strong, prime natural areas can coexist with large cities. Equally important for our purposes, World's End is also a superb destination for walkers just a short drive from the city center.

Traveling from the north or south on I-93, leave the interstate south of Boston at Exit 12 and follow MA 3A *east* to Hingham. Along the waterfront in Hingham you will have views across Hingham Bay to World's End. About 0.5 mile *east* of the Hingham shopping district, watch for Summer Street on your left. Turn *left* off MA 3A onto Summer Street and follow it about a mile *northward* to a cross street. Go across this road diagonally to the *left* onto Martin's Lane. Follow Martin's Lane for 0.75 mile to the reservation gate. Limited parking is available outside the gate and inside past the guardhouse. Arrive early on summer holidays and weekends to be sure of a parking place. An admission fee is charged to support reservation maintenance.

A number of interesting walks meander through World's End. One loop circles Rocky Neck, a ledgy, wooded point of land more typical of the northern New England coast. Another loop circles the large marsh in the peninsula's southern end and is an excellent hike for bird-watchers. The route described here takes the walker over three of the prominent summits within the park and affords excellent water views both in the immediate vicinity and back toward the Boston skyline. This walk is a little less than 2 miles and can be done in a relaxed two hours.

Begin this trip at the guardhouse and walk northwest along the edge of the marsh. There are good views east here over the marsh and west over a human-made dike toward Hingham Harbor. The dike was constructed to make draining of the marsh possible so that salt hay might be harvested. The road on which you are walking goes briskly uphill through red cedar, red pine, and maple. Curving more northward, the road runs over an open heath with more harbor views to the west and northwest. This rise is Pine Hill. Opposite it to the left are Sarah Island and Langlee Island in Hingham Harbor.

The road next pulls northeast, continuing upward, with a low stone wall on the right. Shortly you come to a junction. Keep right here and continue uphill past a field dotted with mixed growth to your right. This leg of the walk soon brings you to the highest point on the peninsula, the summit of Planter's Hill. Fine views northwest over Boston Harbor and of the Boston skyline open up along this stretch. To the east is the Weir River and, beyond it, the sandbar, or tombolo, that forms Nantasket Beach. The small community of Hull lies to the northeast around the towers of WBZ radio.

From the high point of Planter's Hill you will see the second drumlin, which forms the outer tip of the peninsula. An unmarked but obvious path leads straight down the hill to the narrow bar that joins the two drumlins. Walk down through the field now to the trail junction and sandbar, watching for large predatory birds that hunt here. One typical spring day I observed a large goshawk hunt the length and breadth of this field for more than an hour.

Cross the sandbar and head uphill to the right as the road climbs the outermost drumlin. Once past the sandbar, take your second left, a path that runs over the top of the hill. The best views of Boston and the harbor islands are from the top of this 90-foot elevation. Slightly lower to the northeast is the more wooded hillock known as World's End. On the ground along the path you may find the prickly brown husks of the horse chestnut, one of several species of trees that line the route.

Walk west off the summit and regain the main road. Turn left and southeast, walking back toward the sandbar connector. Descending to water level, you may wish to take time out to explore the water's edge. The cove on the Weir River side of the bar usually plays host to a variety of resident and migratory shorebirds. At the trail junction at the foot of Planters Hill, keep left and follow a road that slabs the hill above the Weir River. This trail runs southeast for about ⅓ mile before turning right in mainly deciduous woods and following the edge of the marsh in a southwesterly direction. Another ⅓ mile beyond the turn you come to a junction with the road you earlier took up Pine Hill. Bear left and southeast here, coming in a few minutes to the guardhouse and your car.

World's End Reservation is open throughout the year. Bird-watching, walking, photography, jogging, and cross-country skiing are encouraged. Swimming and picnicking are prohibited.

21 · Ipswich River Wildlife Sanctuary

Location: Topsfield, Massachusetts
Distance: 2⅓ miles
Walking time: 1½ hours

Massachusetts Audubon Society's Ipswich River Wildlife Sanctuary is a first-class, protected reservation embracing a varied area of unspoiled, wild terrain barely 20 miles from Boston at the fringes of one of the nation's largest conurbations. This 2,400-acre preserve, with miles of excellent hiking paths, offers the day-tripper many hours of interesting walking in a scenic, wooded environment.

The Ipswich River Wildlife Sanctuary is a successful example of the important, ongoing efforts of private citizens and conservation groups alike dedicated to the preservation of large tracts of wild land in the shadow of major cities. With the increasing uninhabitability of some of our urban areas, the importance of nearby natural zones as places to walk, observe nature, and spiritually refresh ourselves has become obvious.

Whether approached from the north or south, Ipswich River Wildlife Sanctuary is reached from US 1 in Topsfield, about 3 miles *north* of its junction with I-95. Drive *east* from US 1 on MA 97 and watch for an Audu-

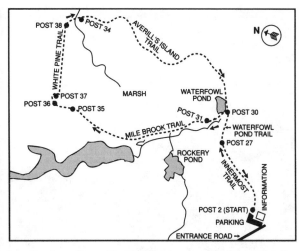

bon Society sign at Perkins Row on your left in 0.5 mile.
Bear *left* on Perkins Row and drive another mile to the
reserve gates on your *right*. A short paved entry road
takes you up through a column of sugar maples in high
meadow to sanctuary headquarters. Park here in the
gravel lot to the *left*.

The walker will find an information board with
notices and maps between the parking lot and the
administration building. Maps can be borrowed or purchased here. Information on birding sites and current
sightings may be acquired at the administration building. A small entrance fee is charged to support upkeep
of the sanctuary and its facilities.

With map in hand, walk to the north side of the
Audubon buildings to post number 2. (All the trails in
the sanctuary are well designated by a series of numbered posts. Letters that mark each trail are usually
attached to nearby trees at trail junctions.) Turn right
and walk down a path that borders an open field and a

row of pole-mounted birdhouses. Here you are on Bradstreet Hill, a glacially shaped drumlin and the highest point in the sanctuary. Make a leisurely stroll downhill to the east, shortly passing a cottage in a grove to the left. Beyond the cottage you arrive at post number 3 and the beginning of the trail marked I, the Innermost Trail. Taking this path, you continue to the northeast now, descending through a corridor of ash scrub populated with busy black-capped chickadees. In a few moments the path enters the woods, meandering through a grove of eastern red cedar and tall white pines. The trail skirts a depression to the right. You come next to a road by a lone northern white cedar that stands astride a small brook at post 19.

Crossing the road, your route is now over a board-walk into a wooded swamp dotted with red maples and birch. By now you have walked from the highest point in the sanctuary to water level in about ¼ mile. Look for a turnout to the right from the boardwalk. A platform at the lip of the marsh provides views of open marsh surrounded by cattails and stunted alder. A bench here makes a good perch for quiet observation of bird life, particularly during the months of migration. Past the turnout, the boardwalk joins the Waterfowl Pond Trail, marked w. Here you go right and east from post number 27. This open woods road will bring you, in a few hundred yards, to a trail junction by Waterfowl Pond, an excellent place to observe ducks and wading birds in-season.

You now turn northward and left across the stone bridge. Dense marsh lies to both the west and north-east. Follow a spongy woods road marked m, the Mile Brook Trail. The brook parallels the trail as it wanders along the west side of an elongated glacial esker. The esker, the low ridge to your right, can be walked if you wish by taking route n from post 31. It rejoins Mile Brook Trail farther on. Eskers, of which there are two north–south examples in the sanctuary, grew through the deposition of rock and gravel by subglacial streams. When the glacial ice sheet receded, these serpentine hills remained.

Passing through spotted alder, white birch, and big white pines, the trail winds northward. At post 35 the trail over the esker comes in from the right. Low hem-locks give way to small clusters of red pine as you begin to climb northward. Plentiful to the north in Maine and New Hampshire, red pine is unusual in the warmer latitudes of coastal Massachusetts. The trail makes an abrupt right turn at post 36. Walking around a corner of the marsh, you turn right again at post 37 onto the White Pine Trail, marked P. The route is now over a high rib in groves of tall, spindly white pines reaching for the sunlight. Small stands of beech are scattered along the trail. Soon the path drops toward the marsh and, at post 38, you turn right over a causeway between two sections of the marsh. A culvert drains one section into the other and, ultimately, into the nearby Ipswich River. Depending on the season, you may hear the rush of water long before you walk across the causeway. Open views of the marsh, particularly fine at sunset, run to the southwest.

Just beyond the causeway at post 34, you make a sharp right into the woods toward the south onto the Averill's Island Trail. This oblong hummock is the second esker and dominates the east side of the marsh, dividing it from the Ipswich River off to the east. The path stays close to the edge of the marsh here. Again you are likely to see ducks and wading birds in-season. The walk now runs under towering beech and hemlock, pulls around to the east, and then goes right and southwest toward Bradstreet Hill. The path is now level as you leave Averill Island and arrive a second time at Waterfowl Pond.

From post 30, cross the intersection and retrace your steps over the route by which you entered. Follow the Waterfowl Trail (W) west to post 27, then go left on the Innermost Trail (I), perhaps stopping once more to watch for bird life in the swamp off the boardwalk. Then simply follow the Innermost Trail uphill, regaining the pasture and the high ground of Bradstreet Hill.

This loop around the sanctuary is less than 2½ miles and can be walked in a leisurely 1½ to 2 hours. The Ipswich River Wildlife Sanctuary has traditionally closed on Monday. Call (617) 887-9264 for information and current hours of opening.

22 · Old Town Hill

Location: Newbury, Massachusetts
Distance: 1½ miles
Walking time: 1 hour

At Old Town Hill in Newbury, the weekend walker will find an elevated lookout above Broad Sound and Plum Island, with additional fine views up and down the northern Massachusetts coast. Old Town Hill is an exception to the general rule that New England's coastal plain is distinguished, in part, by its flatness. Excluding several low mountain ranges in Maine, most of the northeastern coastal corridor is, indeed, characterized by marshlands and sedimentary lowlands. Thus, it's always a treat to walk the occasional high ground wherever hills are found along the coast, for they provide rare opportunities to look *down* and *along* the seascape and to enjoy a unique perspective over the countryside. Old Town Hill just south of Newburyport is just such a place, an easy drive from Boston and only a short distance from Newburyport center. Close by, you'll find other walks on Plum Island.

Old Town Hill is reached by driving *east* and *south* from the junction of State Street and MA 1A in Newburyport. Passing many stately old homes along MA 1A, you soon cross the town line into Newbury. Rounding a long bend, watch for Newman Road on the *right*, 3.5

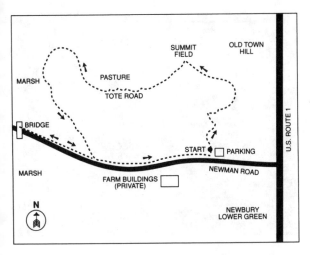

miles south of your starting point. Newman Road runs
along the north side of an attractive lawn known as
Newbury Lower Green. An old schoolhouse stands at its
center, and several magnificent colonial-period houses
border the green. Turn and follow Newman Road a
short distance *west* and park on the shoulder of the road
by a large sign indicating the entrance to the pathway
on the *right*.

Old Town Hill is a 370-acre reservation managed by
the Trustees of Reservations, an organization that oversees 71 preserves in the Bay State comprising more than
17,500 acres. The hill itself is a perfect example of a
drumlin, an elongated or oval-shaped hill created by
glacial deposition. Once farmed (as some of the nearby countryside still is), the hill has been largely over-
taken by dense woods.

Step through the stile at the rock wall by the road
and climb north and northeast on a path that winds
back and forth through groves of red cedar. There are no

signs once you leave the road, but the route is well worn and obvious. The rise is steep but short and, after making several loops up the southeast flank of the hill, you soon pull around to the west, walking through more young cedar and clumps of prickly ground juniper. It is rare to see groves of cedar like these anywhere today, and this stand of *Juniperus virginiana* probably owes its survival to this being protected ground. Passing through a brief depression, the trail rises northwestward, and you shortly arrive in the summit pasture.

Here are the best views on the walk. How much you can see is subject to how recently brush has been mowed back here from year to year. You will spy the camelback of Mount Agamenticus on the far horizon in Maine, its lumpish shape the highest point on the shoreline to the northeast. Above the mouth of the Merrimack is the New Hampshire shore, and due east over Broad Sound lies the long expanse of Plum Island. The sound is fed from the north by the Plum Island River and from the west by the Parker and Rowley Rivers.

Broad Sound and its tributary rivers and streams, together with the barrier beach of Plum Island and its southern tip, Bar Head, constitute one of the more important estuarine areas on the New England coast. This area is home to an impressive variety of marine, animal, and avian species. Around to the southeast are the marshes and dunes of the Ipswich area and Ipswich Bay. Far across the bay to the southeast lie the granite headlands of Rockport at the outer edge of Cape Ann. Although this spot under the old, dying elm of Town Hill is only 168 feet above sea level, its coastal views make it seem much higher. Hardly surprising is the local legend that this spot was used for signaling sailing ships off Cape Ann, for lanterns or fires at this elevation were visible far to seaward.

You now turn west and walk an old woods road that meanders through groves of white pine, poplar, and gray birch. Deer, fox, and raccoon live in these woods, and it is not uncommon to see them if you proceed quietly. You soon pass an opening to another pasture on your right and then go through a stone wall, coming to a clearing with excellent views southwest. The Little River watershed, which is part of a complex marsh system, is seen to the southwest and west.

Beyond this pleasant open area, the road runs northwest and shortly pulls to the right and around the lower end of the second pasture by another stone wall. Birch, maple, and scattered oak grow along the path. A turn is soon made downhill toward the northwest as the trail moves toward the Little River marshes. In minutes you bear left and southwest again, rising through shagbark hickory, downed birch, and the occasional cedar. Following a stone wall, the road pulls farther to the west and reaches a gate above the paved road.

You can simply go left on Newman Road here and walk back to your car, but a right turn will take you quickly to the marshes, which are worth visiting at any time of year. Bear right and walk just over ¼ mile to open marshland. In summer the two immediate bridges along Newman Road provide interesting glimpses through the cordgrass, needlerush, and glasswort to the inner life of the marsh. Many species of birds summer here, and the brilliant white plumage of the snowy egret is a likely sight along the periphery of the river channels. In winter the marsh is snow and ice covered. The ice often blocks drainage of the marsh; ice jams form at the outlets, and the road becomes completely or partially submerged. If you find the road in a submerged condition, use caution. It is advisable to limit your walk to the second bridge, turning around at that point. The road beyond the second bridge may be covered by water to a depth that makes walking or driving hazardous.

When you've inspected the marsh (birding glasses are very useful here), retrace your steps along Newman Road. Through the trees to the right are fine views of pasture that slopes to the Little River watershed. Several old houses and horse barns are passed, and you reach your starting place about ¾ mile from the second bridge. The entire round trip over the hill, down to the marshes, and return is about 1½ miles and can be done in not much more than an hour.

For more information about this preserve and others, write to: The Trustees of Reservations, 572 Essex Street, Beverly, MA 01915.

23 · Parker River National Wildlife Refuge

Location: Newburyport, Massachusetts
Distance: 2 miles
Walking time: 1½ hours

Backed by Plum Island Sound and fronting on the open Atlantic, Parker River National Wildlife Refuge, or simply "Plum Island" as locals refer to it, is an exceptional barrier beach offering miles of superb walking. The refuge contains a 4,600-acre primitive area located on the southern half of Plum Island and surrounding marshes, dunes, beaches, and waterways. A short drive from almost anywhere on the North Shore or Boston area, the Parker River National Wildlife Refuge makes a superb weekend walking destination in any season.

Plum Island itself is one of the East Coast's premier barrier beaches. Discovered by the French explorer Samuel de Champlain in 1601, it appears in detail on the maps of the Englishman Captain John Smith by 1616. The island was used for fruit gathering (wild beach plums) and grazing until the late 1730s. Salt-marsh haying continued into the 1850s. By the end of the 1800s a horse-drawn trolley traveled to the island, and gradually the northern dunes became heavily settled. In the 1930s the Massachusetts Audubon Society managed to save a 1,600-acre plot of land from destructive development by creating a bird sanctuary, which later became a part of the refuge on its opening in 1942.

The Parker River preserve is highly important from an ecological standpoint. More than three hundred different avian species visit the marshes and, according to refuge publications, as many as twenty-five thousand ducks and six thousand geese may be present at the height of migratory periods. Double-crested cormorants, great blue herons, common loons, northern harriers, American kestrels, least terns, sanderlings, and red-breasted mergansers are all readily discovered in the refuge lands. Freshwater pools with bottom vegetation attractive to many species are formed by more than 2 miles of dikes. The refuge also embraces nearly 80 acres of pasture that shelter rabbit and deer as well as provide fodder for large populations of Canada geese.

The refuge is reached from I-95 in Newburyport by taking the MA 113 exit and following it *eastward* toward town, shortly joining MA 1A. Continue eastward on MA 1A, watching for signs indicating the road to Plum Island and the refuge. The approach follows the south banks of the Merrimack River, crosses the Plum Island River, and then makes a *right* turn at the first intersection on the island. Just a short distance south of this intersection is the refuge gate, where information and maps are usually available. An entrance fee is charged when the gate is staffed. Visitors can pay a one-day, per-carload fee to enter. A much better idea is to purchase a current duck stamp, which then becomes your pass to this or any other national refuge for one year. If you visit refuge areas often, the duck stamp pass is much the more economical way to go, and its purchase helps support conservation efforts.

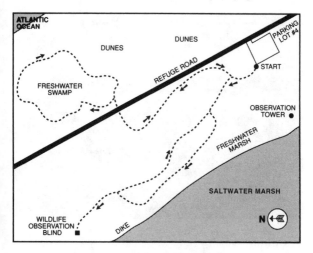

Head south on the refuge service road toward Lot 4, trailhead for the Hellcat Swamp Nature Trail, your destination. As you drive, you may see waterfowl activity to your right in the marshes that line the meandering Plum Island River. Many aquatic birds rest and feed here during their migrations. White-tailed deer are often visible as they graze in open clearings back from the road. There are occasional turnouts where you may pull off the road and park while bird-watching. Three and one-half miles south of the entrance gate you come to Lot 4 on your *right*. Parking in this lot is reserved exclusively for those using the nature trail.

The Hellcat Swamp Trail makes two large, connected loops through densely grown marsh and over primary dunes and interdune areas for an excellent sampling of some of the different kinds of terrain that characterize the refuge. The 2-mile trail begins at the northwest corner of Lot 4 by a post where maps of the route can usually be found. The trail soon becomes

boardwalk, which you follow for just a few yards to the northeast before coming to a junction. Keep left here and take the path that in moments arches left again through the freshwater marsh.

You will soon find yourself, particularly in summer, in a world of giant cattails taller than you are, creating a tunnel-like effect on both sides of the boardwalk. This is a human-made freshwater swamp that provides ideal feed and habitat to many of the species that live here or migrate through this range. Muskrats seem to like the watery terrain beneath the walkway and up the little side eddies in the reeds. Phragmites (reeds) and purple loosestrife grow in abundance. This section of the walk shortly comes to a T, where you bear left and walk northward to the observation blind. If you walk quietly, you'll enjoy the seasonal bird sightings possible from this spot. The blind is right on a bend of the river, so you may spot some of the many geese, ducks, swans, bitterns, herons, and ibises that frequent this area. Bring your binoculars.

Retracing your steps southward, keep your eyes open for tree-nesting birds in the scrub that crowds the walkway. I have observed at close range both short-eared owls and snowy owls here in winter, but you must look carefully, so perfectly are the short-eareds hidden in the thick cover. The snowys tend toward treetops, posts, and roofs as perches.

Pass the boardwalk on which you came into the marsh and continue south as the walk comes to drier ground. At the next junction bear sharply left to walk the second loop. The trail passes through a sunken cedar grove and emerges onto the auto road. Cross the road directly and resume your walk by staying right at the trail junction. The route next drops into a swampy depression thickly grown with speckled alder and other deciduous shrubs. These protected thickets provide good cover and browse for deer.

The boardwalk now climbs to the top of a 50-foot dune where there are excellent views of the ocean. Here you can get a real sense of the varying terrain that makes up the elongated spit of land known as Plum Island. From the water's edge the land is composed of the beach (which rises to a wrack line); the primary dune area, broken by overwashes; the interdune area on which the road is located; and finally the freshwater marshes and, beyond the dikes, saltwater marsh. Sprinkled north and south are stabilizing greenbelts of maritime forest. Beach grass, *Ammophila breviligulata*, grows wild over the dunes, lacing together and anchoring the unstable soil. This sandy turf is extremely fragile and should not be walked upon.

The route next passes a swampy area grown up with bayberry, woodbine, blackberry, and plenty of poison ivy. Black cherry, willow, aspen, and more speckled alder grow in this wet ground. Winterberry, blueberry, serviceberry, and arrowwood also grow here.

Descending gradually, the trail rejoins the road. Bear left and walk south here for a few yards to the parking lot where you left your car. This entire walk can be done in about an hour and a half and is most interesting during April, May, September, and October, when migratory birds may be present in numbers.

24·Bar Head, Plum Island State Reservation

Location: Newburyport, Massachusetts
Distance: 1 mile
Walking time: 1 hour

On Newburyport's Plum Island, at the extreme southern tip of an 8½-mile-long barrier beach and below the southern limits of the Parker River National Wildlife Refuge, lies a relatively rare, elongated coastal drumlin perched right on the shore of the Atlantic. Bar Head, as it is called, is a glacially deposited hill shaped by the retreating Wisconsin ice sheet more than eleven thousand years ago. The drumlin now forms the center of Plum Island State Reservation.

Bar Head and its surrounds form a pleasant wooded upland with water on three sides and terrain well worth some exploration on foot in almost any season. The head offers visitors a perch from which to view the shoreline and open water to the south, and enough hill-and-dale trail walking and beachcombing to satisfy the most inveterate shore lover. The walk is only a mile in length, but the variety of terrain and vegetation seen, along with a great variety of intertidal life and bird species, makes this an absorbing walk of one to several hours' duration in the heart of the 72-acre reserve.

Plum Island State Reservation is reached from Newburyport via Plum Island Road and the Parker River National Wildlife Refuge. An admission fee is charged (see Walk 23: Parker River National Wildlife Refuge, above). Drive the length of the refuge road from the main gate to Lot 7, the southernmost parking area on the island. Walkers are advised to arrive early, particularly in summer months, when the lot may be filled by as early as 10 AM (congestion is not a problem in autumn, winter, or spring, except on occasional weekends). The trailhead is located at a large signboard with trail maps and information on the reservation. A second parking lot is down a dirt road to the right of the signboard.

The walk begins by following a path eastward toward the ocean. This short path is just outside the national refuge boundary, but the distinctive barrier-beach terrain that characterizes the southern half of Plum Island is easily visible northward from here. Plum Island is one of several major barrier beaches along the Atlantic coast. Such terrain is highly fragile, protected only by the thin layer of scattered grasses and other vegetation that anchors the dunes and keeps them from migrating with the stiff winds that buffet the area. Please stay on trails or beach corridors when walking.

You emerge in a couple of minutes on the majestic beach that runs the full length of the refuge's ocean side. Turn to the right and pass a series of tidal pools, watching for the route over Bald Head, which runs southwest. A number of marine species live in this intertidal zone. Rockweed, kelp, Irish moss, and sea lettuce are common. Sea stars and sea urchins, moon snails, common periwinkles, and hermit and green crabs can be seen also.

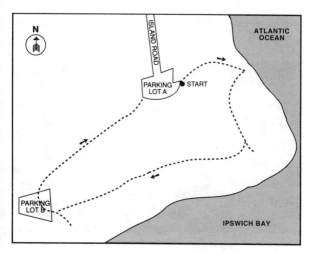

The trail rises over a sandy dune grown up with beach grass, dusty miller, and prolific clumps of goldenrod. As you climb higher, this sandy cover gradually gives way to the soil of the drumlin that underlies it. The drumlin, made up of a heavier soil broken down from the glacial rubble that makes up this hill, provides an anchor for the dune. The going becomes rather steep in minutes as you ascend through dense clumps of white bayberry and poison ivy. These tough bushes are just some of a number of species here that are notably resistant to wind, salt spray, and less-than-perfect soil conditions.

The route levels off soon, passing through a grove of honeysuckle. Staghorn sumac, with its distinctive red horn of berries in-season, and stands of wild cherry border the trail in this section. Continuing over the summit, you arrive at a fine outlook just off the main path. Plum Island Sound is around to the right or west; Ipswich Bay is directly before you. Halibut Point is 7½

miles to the southeast. Hog Island and Crane Beach lie to the south. Castle Hill, a drumlin that lies somewhat back from the shore, is more to the right. This is an excellent spot to relax and observe shorebirds before proceeding.

Back on the main path, you walk farther westward. A second outlook with good views over Plum Island Sound to Great Neck and Little Neck in Ipswich is reached in minutes. You next begin a gradual descent to the shoreline, walking down Bald Head's west slope. Watch for a side trail that takes you out to the beach on your left. This is the protected side of the hill, where the absence of rough breezes directly off the open ocean makes it possible for wild roses *(Rosa rugosa)* and beach plums to prosper. From about midsummer onward the rosebushes are heavy with cherry-sized fruit, or rose hips, as they are commonly named. Dried, ground rose hips are used in many herbal teas and provide a rich source of ascorbic acid, or vitamin C. You may wish to spend some time exploring the water's edge. Winter or summer, the beach seems to collect an interesting assortment of sea wrack washed up here from the open ocean.

Passing a parking lot, you walk northeast on a sandy road. A large freshwater marsh lies off to the northwest. Cordgrass, cattails, and rushes grow densely in this boggy depression. A number of heron and egret species work the shallows, which are also populated with muskrats. The marsh soon gives way to a wooded corridor. Willows, red maples, and speckled alders thrive in this sheltered back corner of the drumlin. Continue through this corridor a short distance to the main parking lot and trailhead where you began the walk.

The route over Bald Head can be done in any season, but walkers should be reminded that hunting is allowed in this reservation for several weeks in autumn. Check with Parker River National Wildlife Refuge headquarters for information. It is prudent not to walk here during the short hunting period. Camping or removal of vegetation is prohibited in the reservation.

IV. New Hampshire

25 · Odiorne Point State Park

Location: Rye, New Hampshire
Distance: 1⅞ miles
Walking time: 2 hours

On the northern edge of New Hampshire's share of Atlantic coast is a band of fine woodland spread along an interesting, beautiful length of shore safe from development. New Hampshire boasts America's littlest saltwater coast, just 18 miles of it. That short coastline has endured more than its share of development, the honky-tonk ugliness of Hampton Beach bearing witness to a thorough disregard for an otherwise beautiful stretch of shore. The addition of a nuclear reactor in the midst of the fragile Seabrook marshes simply compounded the environmental insult to New Hampshire's limited coastline. Luckily, there are corners where attractive woods and shore coexist quietly, safe from the developer's plow.

Odiorne Point State Park provides a number of pleasant walks of varying length and, except on warm weekends in late spring and summer, the trails are largely deserted and tranquil. Though only a few miles from the center of Portsmouth, Odiorne Point provides cover for many bird and animal species, and the amateur naturalist will find much of interest while tramping these woods and coves. The park supports varied, food-rich habitat for both native and migrating bird species, and fox and fisher den here close to the marshes and lowlands. Those same leeward marshes are home to a number of hawk species, particularly redtails and northern harriers,which may be seen occasionally from the trails on the park's west side.

Odiorne Point State Park lies off NH 1A in Rye. From the Portsmouth rotary adjacent to I-95 take the US 1 Bypass *south* to Elwyn Road, opposite Yoken's Restaurant. Go *left* and east on Elwyn Road, shortly joining NH 1A. Follow NH 1A eastward to the *second* entrance on your left to Odiorne State Park. A large parking lot is to the right inside the main gate. Most of the year, entrance to Odiorne is free. A small admission charge is levied May through September.

This walk scribes a figure-eight through the center of the park; it begins to the left of the new Seacoast Science Center, a rangy structure now used to house a variety of nature exhibits. Walk west a few yards on the paved road from the science center and enter the woods on a marked, obvious trail that stays with the shore. This trail is walked westward through groves of aspen and alder scrub, with excellent views across the cove toward Newcastle. As you walk you pass through tall, dense staghorn sumac, black birch, and more aspen. A stone wall, half buried in bittersweet, lies to the right of the path. Passing several trails that depart to the left, you arrive in minutes in an open clearing at a point overlooking a broad cove. A woods road runs to the left, another straight ahead, and a path takes you to the long, rocky strand that follows the shore to the northwest.

This is an excellent spot to look for shorebirds, which can be seen in the cove throughout the year, rid-

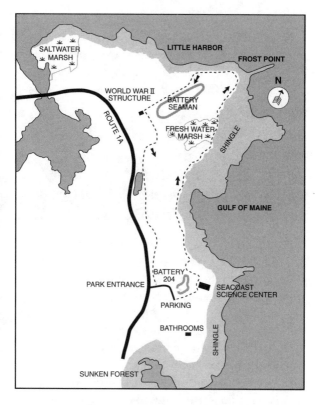

ing out the weather in these relatively sheltered waters. Besides the omnipresent herring gull, common goldeneyes, buffleheads, mergansers, mallards, blue-winged teals, ringnecks, and greater scaups are seen here, particularly in the colder months. Grebes, loons, and yellowlegs are sometimes alongshore. Red-tailed and red-shouldered hawks, northern harriers, and goshawks are regularly spied over the land toward the road, though the encroachment of humans on nearby marshes has reduced the hawk population in recent years. Pairs of

American kestrels may occasionally be seen.

From this high bluff, follow the shingle along the water's edge to the northwest. The walk here is over stones of all shapes and sizes that have been relentlessly ground and polished by the constant action of the tides. To the left is a small freshwater marsh that provides further sheltered cover for shorebirds. Over the marsh is Battery Seaman, a hilly embankment that once formed part of Fort Dearborn's fortifications (you passed a similar fortification, Battery 204, when you walked from your car to the science center). As you walk, the shore gradually pulls in and around to the left and west. The riprap is often littered with ruined lobster traps and other oceanborne detritus washed up here in storms. Fort Stark is on the point across the channel to the right.

If you stay with this shore path as long as you can, you will come to some ledges that you climb over, bringing you to a large field and the breakwater at Frost Point. Red cedar and a few big northern red oaks dot the field, but the ground is mainly open, and there are good views up and down the channel here. This spot, because of its obvious merits as a place from which to fish, farm, or police the waters, has an interesting history. The Italian explorer Giovanni da Verrazano, then in the employ of France, anchored here in 1524. Martin Pring, captain of the English ship *Speedwell*, is believed to have landed here in 1603. The French explorer Samuel de Champlain was off Frost Point in 1605, as was, in 1614, Captain John Smith of the Massachusetts Bay Colony.

In 1623 David Thomson and a party of 10 arrived on the ship *Jonathon* out of Portsmouth, England, and established the small settlement known as Pannaway. This fortified house, situated on a reliable freshwater supply, was probably located near Odiorne Point. From 1759 to 1799 the George Frost farm was located here on the channel, and there is a record of John Foye operating a boardinghouse on the point around 1800. A fine seasonal residence was built here in 1871–72, but the building burned to the ground almost immediately after construction.

The salt marshes to the southwest provided hay for grazing and thatch for the roofs of early cottages. Most settlers engaged in fishing, farming, and trading, and a major fish-processing operation was early established offshore at the Isles of Shoals. John Odiorne, for whom the point is named, worked as a fisherman and blacksmith here after selling a fish business he had set up on the shoals. In 1942 most of the land now in the park became Fort Dearborn, which was taken over by the state in 1961. Forts Stark and Constitution, across the river in Newcastle, were later acquired by the state as well. Dearborn was equipped with 16-inch guns to defend the entrance to the Piscataqua during World War II, and the remains of the giant gun emplacements can be found today.

Follow the shore along the west side of Frost Point. A sandy beach makes up this side of Little Harbor. Fish crows and kestrels may be seen occasionally in the trees here. The long inlet of water that runs southwest from Little Harbor is Witch Creek, which, in turn, is fed by Seavey Creek. Across the water are the towers of the old Wentworth resort. Shortly, you come to a series of paths that cut up the bank to the left and return to the grassy road, which runs along the west side of the gun emplacements. This is the remains of an old military service road, and you walk south on the road, watching for a four-way crossing about 1/4 mile south. Turn left on this road in an open place under some giant red pines and walk east again around a bend and then through a corridor of majestic old maples. Stay on this road as it meanders through mixed-growth woods back to the high bluff where you took to the shingle. From here, bear right and south on the grassy road that runs in the direction of NH 1A (Pioneer Road). You walk now through a typical mixed-growth upland forest in which black-capped chickadees, mockingbirds, and blue jays are year-round residents. The stealthy walker may also see the occasional ring-necked pheasant and partridge here. After a short walk up this corridor, you emerge in an open field, where you bear *immediately* east (left) on a path through the swale. Continue in the open on this path, then through a grove of tall spruce and into another field. Walking a little farther, you soon emerge by the entrance road to the park, with the parking lot just beyond. The entire round trip around the figure-eight is less than 2 miles.

Visitors to Odiorne are encouraged to arrive in the off-season months. From October to May you have the park mostly to yourself. Careful walking in some of the trailed but unmarked sections of the park around by Witch Creek may pay dividends in animal sightings. I have seen gray fox and fishers here in winter. Cottontail rabbits and deer are common as well. After snowstorms, many of the trails in the park can be cross-country skied.

If you are interested in helping preserve and protect the unique woods and shorelands that make up Odiorne Point, contact the New Hampshire Division of Parks, the New Hampshire Audubon Society, or the Friends of Odiorne Point, all of which are active in supporting and maintaining the preserve.

26 · Fort Constitution and Great Island Common

Location: Newcastle, New Hampshire
Distance: 1¼ miles
Walking time: 1½ hours

A jaunt around the Newcastle shore beckons for its fine views of a river mouth and ship traffic, and of the grand Isles of Shoals, visible several miles to seaward. The town of Newcastle is itself an island just out from Portsmouth, connected to the mainland by bridges and causeways along which NH 1B runs. The town is bordered on one side by the Piscataqua River, by the open Atlantic on the east, and by Little Harbor and a series of inlets and small bays on the south and west.

Newcastle is an old settlement, incorporated in 1693, and, given its highly strategic location at the mouth of the Piscataqua, the tiny community has, not surprisingly, played an interesting role in coastal history. The remains of old Fort Constitution occupy the point of land where the Piscataqua meets the sea, and a busy U.S. Coast Guard installation generates a lot of waterside activity just upriver from the fort. All of these can be seen in a short, pleasant walk of less than 2 miles that circles the old town center. This route can be

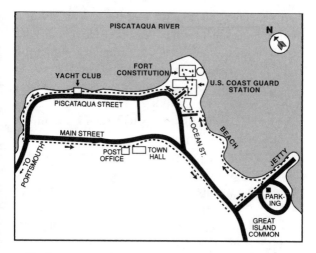

walked any time of year, but a sunny, brisk day in spring or fall is ideal. If you visit in summer, the walk can be capped with a swim at Newcastle Beach at Great Island Common.

Though the town of Newcastle includes several islands within its boundaries, Great Island accommodates most of the settlement. Great Island Common is the name given to the attractive park that slopes down to the sea on the east side of NH 1B (Wentworth Road) just east and south of the town hall. The common is open during daylight hours throughout the year. An entrance fee is charged in high summer, which gains the user access to parking, picnic facilities, showers, and toilets.

Start your walk here with a stroll out to the jetty that leans into the river to the northeast. Across the mouth of the Piscataqua is the site of Fort Foster on Gerrish Island, Maine. To its right out on the ledges lies a rather Victorian-looking house, a former Coast Guard building. Farther still to the right is Whaleback Light, which warns sailors away from the long arc of partially submerged ledges that form the eastern edge of the channel. To your immediate left is automated Newcastle Light next to Fort Constitution and the U.S. Coast Guard base. The first lighthouse on this point of land was built by Governor John Wentworth in 1771. The structure, a wooden tower, was replaced by the current steel turret in 1877. From your position on the jetty you can, on a clear day, enjoy the unusual experience of seeing *four* lighthouses. Newcastle and Whaleback are obvious and usually visible even in murky weather. Far to the northeast beyond Whaleback, Boone Island Light may sometimes be spotted, and around to the southeast is the pretty spire of White Island Light at the southern tip of the Isles of Shoals.

From the jetty, walk ashore and then right to the two small strips of sand known as Newcastle Beach. The beaches form the western edge of a small, rocky bay where a variety of ducks and gulls gather, and cormorants are often seen. Windswept and solitary in winter, the beach is crammed with sun worshipers in summer; your walk along the sands is best scheduled for early morning if you stroll here in June, July, or August. Proceeding to the end of the beaches, turn left and walk up Ocean Street to Wentworth Road. Bear right here and walk the few yards to the entrance road of Fort Constitution and the Coast Guard station. The fort lies behind the Coast Guard buildings at the far end of the drive.

Walking toward the fort, you'll see some of the old fortifications fenced off on your right. These include a Walbach Tower, one of several constructed along the Atlantic shore. These unusual fortifications, rather like the beehive fortresses of the Celtic world, were designed by John de Barth Walbach, a Frenchman who joined the U.S. Army and rose to the rank of brigadier general in the 1790s. The tower was constructed in the War of 1812 and abuts the granite mass of the Farnsworth Battery, an elaborate gun emplacement put up in 1897. Continue on to the portcullis, which forms the main entrance of Fort Constitution. Castle William and Mary was the British name for this outpost. Earthen fortifications here date from 1632, with further additions and improvements being added in the early 1700s.

Some argue that the castle was the site of the Revolutionary War's first skirmish. In December 1774 Paul Revere rode from Boston to warn revolutionaries in Portsmouth of impending hostilities with the British. On December 14 a local band of patriots led by John Langdon and John Sullivan stormed the castle and overpowered the handful of British who were in charge. Weapons and powder were seized to support the revolutionary cause. Today the fort, with its various powder magazines, ramparts, and guardhouses, is very much worth a leisurely exploration. Pamphlets describing the fort are usually available in a box just inside the main gate. The installation became federal property in the early 1790s, but was returned to New Hampshire as a state park in 1961.

Emerging from the park grounds, walk back to Wentworth Road and keep right (in the direction of the river), taking Walbach Street west along the Piscataqua. Walking past several fine houses that date from the late 1600s and early 1700s, you have an opportunity to observe the active river traffic on the Piscataqua. Oil and gas are moved up this river in large tankers. Freighters bring cargoes of salt to the docks in Portsmouth. Scrap steel is shipped down the river on its way to Taiwan for fabrication, and, of course, submarines and workboats attached to the Portsmouth Naval Shipyard also approach through these waters. Three very active yacht clubs have bases along this stretch of river, and sailing activity flourishes here in-season.

If you turn from Walbach Street onto Piscataqua Street, you can continue your walk west through the old village. Many houses date from the revolutionary period or earlier. The Portsmouth Yacht Club is soon passed on the right. As you climb westward slightly, views of the old naval prison open up. This now remodeled structure earned the name of the Castle for its forbidding architecture. Located on the banks of the Piscataqua, the prison was surrounded by water on three sides. No escapee ever succeeded in swimming the river's vicious currents.

Piscataqua Street soon bears left, and you come shortly to Main Street at its bend. Turn left and east here and walk back toward the center of the village, passing the post office and stately town hall. Continue eastward on NH 1B as it pulls to the right. In a few minutes you will arrive at the entrance to Great Island Common and your starting point. Allow $1\frac{1}{2}$ to 2 hours for this walk, giving you ample time to explore Fort Constitution.

V. Maine

27 · Mount Agamenticus

Location: York, Maine
Distance: 1 mile
Walking time: 1½ hours

Although there are occasionally hills and low mounds along the southern New England coast, the real coastal mountains begin in Maine. The raised, rounded upland that you notice slightly to landward from almost anywhere on the southern Maine coast is Mount Agamenticus, a 700-foot elevation that ascends in woodlands to the west of the Yorks. The ledgy whaleback is the first of a series of low hills that march northwestward toward the more substantial ranges inland.

Surrounded by sea-level terrain, a mountain right on the coast doesn't have to be very high to provide splendid views, and this Agamenticus does nicely. In fact, if you want a first-class aerial view of the coast from just south of Portland all the way down to Portsmouth, New Hampshire, Agamenticus is indisputably the best walk of that kind in southern Maine.

To begin your walk on Agamenticus, locate York on a map and drive north or south on US 1 to York's Cape Neddick section. (York can also be reached via I-95.) On the west side of US 1, where the road makes a bend by an old farmhouse, go *west* on Mountain Road (sometimes called Agamenticus Road). Follow this winding

163

road west for about 1.3 miles to a point where it meets Chase's Pond Road. Keep *right* at the junction and continue westward, staying *left* next at a pronounced Y near an old schoolhouse that you'll come upon soon. About 2¾ miles from the junction with Chase's Pond Road, you run out of pavement where Mountain Road suddenly becomes gravel. Just before this spot, where the paved road turns uphill, is a gravel parking area on the *right*. Leave your car here, well off the road and also out of the way.

The Ring Trail runs from the parking area signboard northward through the woods on what was once an old tote road. This area has been actively logged in recent years. Eight public and private landowners now control the 7,000 acres that surround Agamenticus and the mountain upland itself. The woods are slowly growing back. The path meanders northward briefly up the rise, staying close to the paved road, and immediately comes to a fork. Here you walk west to the paved road, follow it northward uphill for a short distance, and reenter the woods on another, more obvious, woods road that arches westward from a small, second parking area.

Unlike the ground you've just covered, which has been nearly cleared of hardwoods, this second woods road lies in dense mixed growth. A canopy of hemlock, fir, and white pine covers the path and holds back sunlight. To the left the land drops off into a depression grown up thickly with alder, beech, white ash, and scattered red cedar. Moose, fox, white-tailed deer, rabbit, and other species live in these woods, and you're likely to spot their tracks along this road as it bends leftward over some wet ground. I once encountered a cowering

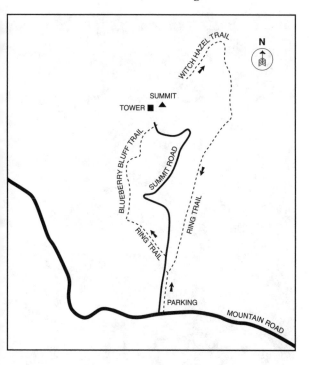

little field mouse here on a snowy day. Not being able to get to his burrow in the frozen ground, he dived under a big leaf and hid there until he heard the clump of my boots receding.

Heads up. Abruptly, the Blueberry Bluff Trail leaves this path and runs northward to the right up the slope. Turn right and ascend northward on steeper ground. The woods thin out now. Low, weather-stressed oaks, some red spruce, and balsam dot the hillside as you walk briskly upward. Limited views southwestward through the trees open up. The route makes a couple of short bends to the right, runs over some fractured

ledge, and emerges on the summit gravel parking area by a paddock and stable.

Agamenticus's summit still shows faded evidence of a long-disused ski area. Summit buildings have become part of the parklands or removed. Stanchions that once supported ski tows stand like lonely sentinels on the north slopes. An imposing cluster of microwave antennas belonging to Mother Bell are beside the paved road to your right. Walk to the former Maine Forest Service tower next to another antenna farm and climb up for some of the excellent views noted earlier. During the summer season, when the tower is staffed, it may be possible to visit the warden's perch. Knock and ask permission. (Visitors to this and other volunteer-staffed towers in Maine will find David Hilton's *From York to the Allagash: Forest Fire Lookouts of Maine* an interesting read. The tower on Agamenticus is one of those recorderd in its pages. Copies can be orderd from David Hilton at 8 Camden Avenue, York, ME 03909.)

To the northwest you will see the rangy mass of Mount Hope in Sanford. When the air is clear, particularly in winter, you may spot Mount Washington and the Presidential Range (over Mount Hope) 100 miles distant. The range is particularly visible when coated with snow in winter. To the west is the relatively flat plain of eastern New Hampshire. Mountains in the Lakes Region of New Hampshire rise to the northwest. Coastal views are equally spectacular from the tower. The point of land far to the northeast is Fletcher's Neck at Biddeford Pool (well beyond the large water tower). Maine's famous beaches at Kennebunk, Moody, Wells, and Ogunquit form the immediate coast to the northeast and east. York, with its fine lighthouse at the Nubble, lies off to the southeast. The thin, lonely spire on the ledges east of York is Boone Island Light. Far around to the south you may be able to make out the fabled Isles of Shoals off Portsmouth and Rye.

Before you leave the summit, you may want to explore some of the old ski trails that drop off the north side of the mountain or new walking trails that are now part of the parklands. A lot of interesting bird life may be spotted in the woods around the summit. Various hawks, turkey vultures, migrating songbirds in-season, and several resident species can be found.

When you're ready to head down, find the Witch Hazel Trail, which runs a short distance northeastward from the summit building. It will bring you to a junction with the Ring Trail. Go right on the Ring Trail and descend southward through groves of mixed hardwoods along the mountain's east flank. The trail pulls slightly to the southwest as it descends and brings you in minutes to the parking area where you first set out.

Agamenticus can be climbed (round trip) in an hour. Wiser heads won't rush it, and will allow at least 1½ or 2 hours for the walk, some summit exploration, and time to enjoy those tremendous outlooks on the New England coast. Except on very warm days, it's a good idea to take a jacket or sweater with you when you climb the summit tower. This little mountain catches a lot of wind, and in even moderate weather it can be chilly on top. In winter the strong winds that roll south from the greater ranges hit the mountain constantly, and the summit can become nearly polar.

28 · Long Island, Casco Bay

Location: Portland, Maine
Distance: 2 to 4 miles (depending on route selected)
Walking time: 1½ to 3 hours

The great, glaciated coastline of Maine, thrust downward thousands of years ago by a giant, mile-thick ice sheet and scrubbed by glacial extension and recession, is naturally blessed with hundreds of islands. Folklore suggests that 365 islands nestle within the confines of Casco Bay, but on closer examination this estimate is, perhaps, too generous. Many of these ledgy masses are just that, and not true islands. Somewhere in the neighborhood of 150 to 160 of the bay's nuisance-rocks-called-isles actually disappear under the surface at high tide and are not true islands at all. Of the remaining 200 or so, perhaps 130 are of habitable size and worthy to be called islands.

All this is quibbling, of course, for within the vast 200 square miles of Casco's waters there rests enough beautiful island terrain to make any such qualification unnecessary. Whatever the final estimate, Casco Bay encompasses a large cluster of *walkable* coastal islands, some easily reached by scheduled boat service from Portland. Luckily for the coastal walker, nice strolls in this archipelago can be done as serene day hikes only minutes away from the bustle of greater Portland. If you like islands—and how could you not—you will enjoy island walking for its uncommon sense of separateness and tranquility. Pretense doesn't fare well on an island. Quiet reigns.

Once settled by Abenaki Indians of the Algonquin Nation, Long Island remains one of the less populated of the big inner islands of Casco Bay. Cottages and simple little houses constitute the limits of development here, and a store, a post office, and a seasonal restaurant are about the limit of amenities on Long. A new dock stands alongside the old one. That's just fine, for where few amenities exist, you find fewer people. The walker can get to Long Island by catching a Casco Bay ferry from the new terminal building at the junction of Franklin and Commercial Streets on the Portland waterfront. Several boats service Long daily, and the idea is to catch an early trip and not come back until late afternoon. For information on sailings, contact the Casco Bay Island Transit District at (207) 774-7871.

The cruise to Long will delight you. Portland still has the vestiges of a working waterfront, and evidence of fishing, shipbuilding, and cargo transfer is all about as the boat heads outward. South Portland's tanker terminals lie to your right, and Fort Gorges hunkers down in the waves to your left as you cross the inner harbor. Before Secretary of War Jefferson Davis quit his post to become president of the Confederacy, he oversaw plans to build this watery fort in 1858. Like those military expenditures of today with which we are so familiar, Fort Gorges was an expensive waste. Changes in naval warfare rendered the fort obsolete even before it was complete, and the granite hulk was never garrisoned.

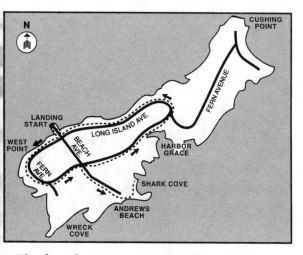

The ferry for Long usually stops at several other islands on its way northward. Peaks Island is often visited first as one of the larger and more populous of these commuter isles. From Jones Wharf at Peaks the boat runs northwest to Little Diamond. You then continue more northeastward, past the hulks at the north end of Little Diamond to the landing on Great Diamond. Lamson Cove separates the two Diamonds, but at low tide you can walk across a connecting sandbar. From Great Diamond it's only a short run farther northeast past Diamond Cove to the landing on the southwest shore of Long Island, where you disembark.

Walk up the grade from the dock and you find yourself on Long Island Avenue, a circular road that loops around the southern two-thirds of the island. Turn right now, walking past a restaurant, the tiny post office, and the general store. (Long is a very seasonal place, and walkers should not count on buying provisions here in the off-season. Pack along your own lunch and water.)

You soon come to an open space and path leading to the water's edge. If you take to the shoreline here, especially at low tide, you can potter along the water's edge, possibly finding some interesting flotsam cast up by the sea. At low tide, mussels and rockweed glisten. Periwinkles dot the exposed rocks in great numbers.

If you stay with the shore you will soon round West Point, where College Island lies off to the south. Watch for a break in the foliage and a road that departs from the high ground to the left and brings you quickly back to Long Island Avenue. Follow the avenue right and east past scattered dwellings to the eastern shore of the island. Asters, common fleabane, dandelions, and goldenrod grow wild in the brush along the road. Pulling to the north on the avenue, you come shortly to Beach and Cushing Avenues, which come in on the left. Go right on Beach Avenue and walk out to Andrews Beach, an attractive stretch of sand and shingle that runs northeast to Andrews Nubble. A walk along the beach will bring you to Shark Cove, a small inlet just beyond the nubble. Obed's Rock is the ledge east of the cove.

To the southeast, just off the beach, lies Vaill Island. Farther away and to the southwest you'll see Overset Island. The inlet between Andrews Beach and Overset has earned itself the name of Wreck Cove. Casco Bay ledges have claimed many a wooden ship, and if you happen to arrive here on a day when the open ocean is running lustily, it won't be hard to imagine how a ship could be driven up on the rocks.

Long has four tiny satellite islands. You'll spot all of them on this walk except Crow Island, which lies off Cushing Point at Long's northern shore. Luckse Sound separates Long from Cliff and Jewel Islands, the two larger shapes to the northeast and east. Other minuscule islands in the area carry such crusty names as West Brown Cow, Ministerial, Rogues, Pumpkin Nob, and Smuttynose. Hope Island lies west of Cliff to the northeast, and Inner Green Island, Green Island Reef, Outer Green Island, and Junk of Pork Island may be barely visible, low in the water, far on the eastern horizon.

Depending on how much time you have, you may wish to go back to Long Island Avenue and follow it north to Harbor Grace and then back south along the leeward side of the island. Allow at least an hour and a half if you head northward. For a shorter return to the dock, retrace your steps on Beach Avenue, cross Long Island Avenue, and continue westward to Long's lee shore. This route will bring you out just above the dock, where you'll pick up the ferry for the return trip.

If you go to Long on a hot day in summer, remember that the ocean side of the island is sometimes a good deal cooler than onshore temperatures. Even on a sunny day it's a good idea to pack along a light sweater or jacket with your lunch in case the winds are making up from the east.

As you ship back to Portland at the end of the day, you may experience a fine sunset over the city's distinctive eastern and western humps, or promenades. Also, in midharbor, if you look over your shoulder back to the southeast, you can take in the big cliffs of Portland Head and its old and famous lighthouse.

29·Fore River Sanctuary

Location: Portland, Maine
Distance: 2¼ miles
Walking time: 1¾ hours

One of those features that have repeatedly landed Portland high on the national list of habitable small cities is the presence of places to walk in natural settings. Ocean frontage, nearby islands, river country, and wooded reserves have helped Portland remain an attractive place not entirely dominated by concrete. In the Fore River basin you'll find an urban escape walk in one of those blessed little havens of woodland close to the city center, all the more attractive for its contrasts.

Fore River Sanctuary lies just inland from Portland Harbor on the west side of Maine's largest urban zone. Comprised of 76 acres of woods, marsh, streams, and hills, the preserve is a pretty, hidden corridor where you can walk in the midst of, yet apart from, the bustle of the city. The sanctuary abuts colonial-era Stroudwater village, and the grounds are thick with history. Most important, this is a sheltered estuarine area where streams and brooks carry rich freshwater effluent from inland to the broader expanses of the Fore River, an arm of Portland Harbor. The marshlands and woods are home to a variety of avian and animal life, and naturalists will find this an interesting walk.

To reach the trailhead, leave I-295 on the Congress Street *west* exit in the center of Portland. Once on Congress Street, make an immediate *right* turn onto Douglass Street, followed by a *left* onto Brighton Avenue. Drive *west* on Brighton Avenue, going through three traffic lights. After passing Capisic Street on your left, slow down and watch for Rowe Avenue (also on your left). Turn *left* onto this street and follow it all the way to the end, where parking is available in a grassy runout.

The trail runs left along some railroad tracks a short distance, and you can see the center of the marsh farther eastward as you walk along this section. Soon you come to a brightly marked crossing where you turn southward and, *using caution,* step over the tracks. The walk now scrambles up a rise covered with white pines and birches, then meanders southeastward through a grove, passing a trail on the right and dropping toward the marsh. In a couple of hundred yards you come to the edge of the marsh, grown up thickly in salt hay. A wooded drumlinlike upland, dotted with trees, lies to the right. Ahead, a boardwalk connects the ridge you are on with another rise across a marshy inlet. Just before crossing the boardwalk, you'll find a good perch to view this segment of the marsh.

Maine Audubon Society, the owner of this unique sanctuary, reports that black ducks and cormorants are common here, as are belted kingfishers, black-capped chickadees, blue jays, and other seasonal nesting birds. Marsh hawks may be seen soaring over the waves of sunken salt hay.

Cross the boardwalk and bear sharply left along the high ground, where you'll find views eastward toward the city. Pulling to the northeast, you cross the railroad

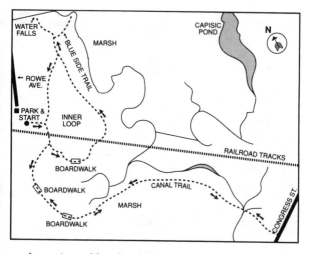

tracks again and head uphill into a hemlock-spruce forest. After passing under the power lines and walking northward on an open path, you soon enter a stand of red oak and beech. The path follows a high rib of land above the more northerly reaches of the marsh.

Continuing northward, you come to a hemlock grove where a trail goes left. Remember this spot; you will follow that other trail on your return. Walking still northward, you reach a blue blaze on a tree where a trail runs to the right along another ridge. This side trail is worth a short detour. It follows this secondary rib northeastward and descends to the edge of the marsh. Good views southeast and west open up here. The path continues out into the marsh, but the going is wet. Halt at this spot.

Retrace your steps up the grade to the top of the rib and head back to the junction where you made your turn, then go right and downhill toward a grove of white pines on a banked and graded path. In just a few

yards you come to something totally unexpected within the confines of a city: a pretty, natural waterfall. One of the feeder brooks that runs into the Fore River skips down over granite ledges here at the very edge of the preserve.

From the falls, walk back up to the hemlock grove you passed through earlier and take the branch trail to the right (southwest). This trail runs toward the railroad tracks through more deciduous forest and returns to the entry trail you traveled from the parking area. At this point you may either bear right and return to your car or embark on a long point-to-point walk into the heart of the marsh, following the old Cumberland & Oxford Canal towpath.

For the towpath walk, go back to the first railroad crossing and cross again to the south. Once in the grove on the opposite side of the tracks, take the trail to the right, which loops southwestward to the marsh, bringing you to a walkway that runs east-southeast along the lowland. Crossing two boardwalks, you hike the Canal Trail, which parallels the now disused waterway.

Built in 1830, the old Cumberland & Oxford is a relic of the days before the railroads. It connected the rich timberlands inland with Portland Harbor and the world of overseas shipping. The canal linked up with a chain of lakes to the north and west, making it possible to bring cargo from Harrison Lake, through Sebago Lake, and down to the Portland wharves. The tall, straight trees of Maine's primeval woods were in demand throughout the world in the era of wooden ships. Millions of board feet of mast timber moved down to Portland and other Maine harbors and thence overseas.

The Canal Trail continues as far eastward as outer Congress Street. Follow it just to the point where it crosses the river, then walk back the way you came. Pass through the woods, cross the tracks, and continue the short distance to your car. The entire walk around the northern loop and down the marsh bottom and back is about 2¼ miles and can be walked in less than two hours.

Spring is perhaps the most interesting season in this sanctuary. Resident otter, raccoon, and muskrat may be seen, as well as woodchuck and deer. Most of all, spring is the time of the great bird migrations along the coast, and Fore River Sanctuary is a protected oasis where migratory birds pause on their journey north. Fall also provides the bird-watcher with some interesting sightings as these migrators head southward.

Hunting and camping are not allowed in the preserve. *Be alert* when crossing the railroad tracks during your visit.

30 · Gilsland Farm Sanctuary

Location: Falmouth, Maine
Distance: 1¼ miles
Walking time: 1½ to 2 hours

Just upriver from Portland Harbor, Maine Audubon Society's Gilsland Farm suggests an excellent half day's exploration through terrain busy with birds and wildlife. This old, rolling farm site is also home to Maine Audubon's headquarters, which occupy one of the pioneering large solar structures in the state. The main building includes a library, meeting facilities, nature exhibits, and a small shop that sells an interesting variety of books, bird feeders, guidebooks, maps, and binoculars. Walkers will find a map of sanctuary trails here, and you may wish to purchase the useful pamphlet *Natural Communities of Gilsland Farm.*

The importance of preserving even small tracts of land along rivers and bays near cities becomes highly apparent when you walk Gilsland's trails. Just next door to Maine's largest city, this preserve offers extensive walking over rolling, moorlike fields, through wooded copses, and along the headlands and marshes of the Presumpscot River. Gilsland consists of three distinct sections: the North Meadow, which borders the mudflats and North Marsh; the central section, with its cultivated grounds, distinctive plantings, and headquarters

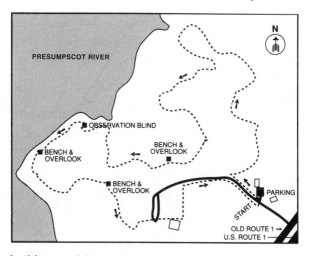

building; and the South Marsh–West Meadow area, bordering the Presumpscot. A long north–south ramble around the perimeter of the sanctuary will introduce you to each of these areas.

Gilsland Farm is just off US 1, diagonally opposite its junction with ME 88 in Falmouth. The entrance is on a small loop road to the *west* of US 1, about 2.5 miles *north* of Portland via Martin's Point. From the paved loop, turn in on a dirt road and park shortly on your *right* between the Energy Education Center and barn.

This walk begins at a path on the north side of the parking area and runs northwest by the barn to a trail junction above the garden. Keep right at this junction and follow the path over high meadow, in a section reminiscent of Scottish moors. The path here is sometimes wet as it meanders north and northwest through the swale, gradually pulling to the west along a bluff above the river. The southwestward views here (before you come to a border of trees) are excellent over the

North Marsh, some mudflats, and the Presumpscot River. Going first south and then east, the path pulls back from this promontory, makes a U-turn, and then marches southwest and then southeast, staying close to the marsh. Distinctively marked bobolinks and killdeer make their nests in these fields and fly busily about, frequently disappearing into the tall grass where they shelter. Meadow voles and woodchucks are abundant.

Having skirted part of the marsh, you continue eastward to a trail junction, where you stay right, descending gradually to a tree-lined depression, and cross a footbridge. The trail now leaves the open meadow and runs southwestward under a wooded canopy of pine, fir, birch, and maple. Red and gray squirrels, skunk, raccoon, woodchuck, red fox, and white-tailed deer move through these woods. Shortly, on your right, you come to a side trail that leads to a settee by the edge of the marsh. For bird-watchers and photographers this spot makes a good platform to watch ducks and other birds, particularly in migratory seasons. Beyond this place, you walk in a more westerly direction, gradually rising to open ground again, pulling north briefly by rows of crab apples, and then going west again along a tree-lined bluff.

Coming to a trail junction, keep right and make a loop along the edge of the marsh, descending to a river blind in a grove of tall oaks. This blind is well situated for those who would like to rest a moment and watch ducks and shorebirds wheel and skirt over the river, often landing in the protected waters directly in front. A short loop trail climbs away from the marsh and back up to the tableland you have been walking. Follow it and walk southwest along the edge of West Meadow. Open views to the east and southeast reveal more bird activity, for the frequently seen killdeer and bobolink nest here, too. On your right is a border of staghorn sumac and quaking aspen, which shortly yields to river outlooks at a point of land where there is a bench. Great blue herons, a variety of ducks, yellowlegs, and snowy egrets work the marshy ground to the south.

From this grove of oaks, walk southeast and east above what is called the South Marsh. You can see downriver all the way to Portland in breaks between the trees. Ragweed and horsetails grow here among more spindly, tough sumacs. The trail rises to a mount and then descends eastward into some boggy woods where maples, birch, and red oak grow. Several varieties of woodferns line the sometimes wet path. Shortly, you rise northeastward, cross a trail, and continue up the banking to emerge in the main parking area. Continue across this lot to the administration building. When you leave the building, take the path out back to the west under a canopy of trees. You'll come in a few moments to the preserve driveway. Take a right here and walk back to your car by the barn and energy education center. As you walk eastward, there are excellent views over marsh and meadow to the river where you walked earlier.

This loop can be walked in about two hours. The walk shouldn't be hurried, and you might allot extra time for sitting in the blinds watching for birds and also for visiting the administration building. Though composed nearly equally of high and low ground, the trails at Gilsland have their wet spots even in high summer. Do wear a pair of well-made, waterproof walking shoes or boots.

31 · Mast Landing Sanctuary

Location: Freeport, Maine
Distance: 1½ miles
Walking time: 1½ hours

Mast Landing and its surrounding woodlands have supported human settlement from the 1700s onward. This unique region supplied timber, particularly ships' masts, to the coasting trade, and a lot of that wood moved through the landing and down the Harraseeket River. A sawmill, two gristmills, and a fulling mill formerly existed within what is now a Maine Audubon sanctuary, all powered by Mill Stream's water, captured behind the ancient granite milldam.

You will see other remnants of human habitation at Mast Landing. In 1795 Abner Dennison, for many years the miller here, built his house on the rise above the milldam, and that dwelling still stands today. At one time cornmeal and animal feed were ground in the mills, lumber was sawn, and cloth woven, all by waterpower. The mills burned around the time of the Civil War and were never reconstructed.

Farming took over this land around the turn of the 20th century, including the introduction of orchard crops. Although the orchards still bear fruit and some of the fields are kept open, much of the land has gone back to dense forest perfect for walking. This combination of orchard, open fields, and thick cover is also precisely what makes this ground so attractive to wildlife. The L. M. C. Smith family presented the sanctuary lands to Maine Audubon in 1962.

Mast Landing Sanctuary today offers an ecologically oriented summer camp for children and is open to walking throughout the year. For children learning about the ecology of place, the 150-acre sanctuary provides an excellent example of a settlement once heavily used by human residents that has now returned to a more natural state. And for those enthused about strolling through beautiful mixed-growth woodlands, spotting riverine wildlife, or who enjoy wild bird observation, Mast Landing will easily become a favorite walking place.

Reach Mast Landing Sanctuary by driving *southeast* and *east* on Bow Street from the center of Freeport, opposite the L. L. Bean store. Shortly, you bear left and northeast, connecting soon with Lower Mast Landing Road. As the road dips into a marshy area above the Harraseeket, watch for Upper Mast Landing Road, where you bear *left* and go up a hill. Cresting the hill immediately, you turn *right* onto a well-marked dirt road into the sanctuary and park in the lot on your *left* as you enter.

A series of trails runs through Mast Landing, and this walk will introduce you to almost all the varying terrains and vegetation in the reserve. It is one of the longer routes for walkers, about 1½ miles in length. The trail begins near a board marker at the north corner of the parking lot. You will follow the Loop Trail, which runs more or less level nearly all the way and makes a circuit of the reserve, returning via the milldam and the

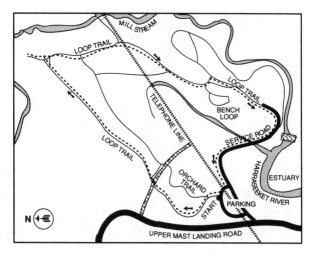

mill master's house. This route also serves cross-country skiers and snowshoers well in winter.

From the parking area, walk north and northwest through old pasture and orchards dotted with apple trees. If you are walking at dawn or just before dusk, you may see deer looking for fallen apples in this area. At the end of the field the trail enters the woods by a grove of young aspens. You next pass two big sugar maples and walk through a stone wall, passing the Cut-Off Trail to your right.

Your route now follows an old woods road, passes a cellar hole among some aspens to the left, and heads north along a shaded ridge. Red oak, beech, and red pine shelter the quiet path. Poplar and black cherry appear in small stands. Right now you are probably at the highest point in the sanctuary. The big trees that join overhead give this section of the trail a roofed-in quality. In moments you begin to descend into balsams, red spruce, and hemlock, coming soon to a little

turnout to the left where a bench has been placed.

If you rest in this quiet corner of the reserve for a moment, you'll find that a surprising amount of bird life exists in this dense evergreen growth. In-season you'll gradually pick up the song of black-throated green warblers, eastern kingbirds, black-capped chickadees, hairy woodpeckers, and others. Barred owls, broad-winged hawks, and great blue herons have been seen in various areas of the sanctuary.

From this resting place, step back to the Loop Trail and head east through a shady grove of very closely grown white pine. Moving generally toward the southeast, the trail runs above a densely vegetated bog through which Mill Stream flows. The high ground hereabouts drains into the bog, which then feeds Mill Stream as it makes its way down to the Harraseeket. The narrow Mill Stream isn't particularly big or impressive as it meanders through the sanctuary, but by the time the Harraseeket flows into the ocean, it has formed a broad bay nearly a mile wide. Mink, beaver, fisher, and muskrat forage along the stream's banks in the northern and eastern quarters of the reserve. Deer come down to drink. The course of Mill Stream may be difficult to see from here in summer's thick vegetation, but you will get a closer look by the milldam later.

You next pass the Deer Run Trail on your right and continue to walk toward the southeast in a long alley of balsam, hemlock, and white pine. You come to the brushy and little-maintained Stream Spur Trail on the left in a moment. This grassy, unmarked trail descends north to the water. If you are interested in streamside ecology and the possibility of spotting some of the small animals that frequent the streambanks, take the time to make this short side trip. On the Loop Trail you pass under a telephone line and turn southward in still denser coniferous forest.

Passing the Bench Loop Trail on your right, you walk easily to the south now where the trail opens out in mixed growth and, turning eastward in a moment, emerges into open pasture. Bear right and march southward again through the remains of an old orchard. The Audubon summer day camp building lies on the right, and you soon come to the mill master's house, which is currently a private residence. To the left and east of the mill master's house is a grassy path that takes you down to the banks of the milldam.

Walk down the road from the mill master's house and take another short side trail on your left out to the milldam. Here you can watch Mill Stream as it tumbles down over the headwall and into the lowland known as the Harraseeket River Estuary. A mere trickle in high summer, the stream runs full with snowmelt and spring runoff. You will also note the progress of the river when you drive down the hill outside the sanctuary. There you can see the progress of the outflow across the marsh and on toward the bay. The dam is now in disrepair, but it's still an interesting bit of work and something of an engineering marvel when you think how primitive were the means by which these great stone blocks were cut and hauled into place so long ago.

Walk westward down the road and over a feeder brook, with the estuary to your left. As the road bends toward the northwest and begins to climb, a side trail runs left out into the estuary. You may follow it if you wish, or stay with the road. The Estuary Trail makes a short loop that then returns to the parking area. With the dam behind you, the road shortly crests the hill and you arrive, on your right, at your starting point.

The entire loop can be made in an unhurried hour and a half. A complete guide to all the trails and natural features of Mast Landing can be purchased from Maine Audubon Society, 118 U.S. Route 1 South, Falmouth, ME 04105. Please note that no trail bikes or motorized vehicles are permitted in the reserve. Camping and fires are also prohibited, in the interest of protecting the sanctuary's unique vegetation.

32 · Wolf Neck Woods State Park

Location: Freeport, Maine
Distance: 1¾ miles
Walking time: 1½ hours

The result of glaciation many thousands of years ago, Maine's deeply scoured and depressed coastline is, in some ways, reminiscent of Norway. Wolf Neck, which this walk traverses, furnishes a fine example of the unspoiled beauty long ago associated with Maine's striated, deepwater coast. Wolf Neck Woods, a Maine state park of some 200 acres, takes the shape of a densely forested band across a narrow peninsula that juts into Casco Bay and the Atlantic. Wolf Neck is one of many thin arms of Maine land that plunge oceanward along the coast and increase its actual length to more than 2,000 miles of bays, inlets, sounds, and coves.

Wolf Neck's woods were donated for public use in 1969 through the thoughtful and generous gift of the Lawrence Smith family of Freeport. Today these parklands are crisscrossed by a web of marked trails that offer inspiring coastal walking in a pristine, bayside environment. Though the park is formally open from late spring through autumn, the striking trails of Wolf Neck Woods can be walked in any season. Cross-country skiing may be pursued on some of the wood's trails in winter.

To visit Wolf Neck Woods, drive *southeast* and *east* on Bow Street from Freeport center, rounding the bend and continuing *northeast* on Flying Point Road. Two and one-quarter miles from the L. L. Bean store, bear *right* off Flying Point Road onto Wolf Neck Road. This rural lane winds southward past a series of small coastal farms and deposits you shortly by the well-marked entrance to Wolf Neck Woods State Park. A small entry fee is charged in high season. If the park is closed and the gate shut, park on the *northbound* side of the paved road, north of the park entrance, and then walk in. When the park is formally open and the gatehouse staffed, ask the attendant for a map of the park to orient you.

Wolf Neck's trails all begin from a common point at the southeast end of the main parking area. (Walk in to this spot if the gate is closed in the off-season.) A large display board shows the various trails and places of interest in the park. Each trail might almost be called self-guiding. Environmental points of interest are well explained by trailside placards as you walk. Plant descriptions, geology, forest growth, erosion, and other subjects are called to your attention along the way. This feature makes Wolf Neck an exceptional walk for the young. You learn here how to *see* what actually goes on in the life cycle of a prime shoreline woodland.

During this walk you will make a complete circle of the grounds. From the display board walk southeast on the Casco Bay Trail. This route runs first on the level through groves of pretty white birch, and the ground lies carpeted in woodferns. Soon you bear left and climb, via a step, over a ledgy area, descending through

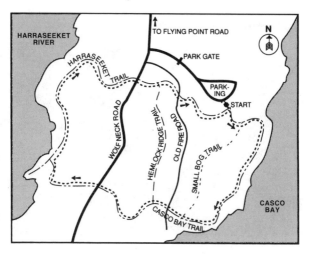

spruce and fir (a good deal of it knocked over by rough coastal winds in places) to the water's edge. A glance to the northeast reveals Googins Island, now preserved as a sanctuary for ospreys. The birds seem to occupy the island on a schedule largely their own. The big tree on the island, once the site of a prominent nest, lost its top in a storm and the nest and newly hatched young with it. Periodically other nests have been constructed. Park officials may be able to apprise you when you enter the park of whether ospreys are nesting on the island.

Below you here on the shore are some dramatic examples of the neck's geological history. Sedimentary rock, laid down millions of years ago by Acadian seas, lies exposed along this stretch of shore, twisted and upfolded, the long cycle of gradual deposition obvious to the eye. You can observe the work of thousands of years of geological activity in an inch or two of layered rock, now swept clean by Maine tides.

Next you walk southwest above the shore, cross a tiny footbridge, and proceed through a grove of young hemlock. About ½ mile from your car you begin to turn west and start the inland walk across the center of the neck. The trail rises over a low hillock into dense groves of evergreens, shortly leveling off as it leads northwest. In this section of the trail you begin to notice the shrubs and plants common to the reserve. Bunchberries, a deep green rosette of leaves topped by brilliant red berries and a white blossom in-season, lie scattered along the side of the path. Partridgeberry, mayflower, and varieties of mosses are often seen.

Passing through a stand of mature white pines, you walk over a hump and down into a depression, cross a fire road, and go under a power line. Continuing westerly, you soon go through an aged stone wall amid more pines, gray birch, red spruce, and hemlock. More bunchberries lie scattered about with their perfect, rich colors. You next meet the Harraseeket Trail coming in on the right. Keep to the left on what now becomes the Harraseeket Trail and continue northwest, climbing down some shaded ledges and entering another depression. In minutes you cross Wolf Neck Road and dip back into cool, dark woods. Moving by a stand of densely grown, impenetrable white pines, you drift down to the high banks above the waters of the Harraseeket. As you descend to the cliffs on the west side of the peninsula, watch for an unmarked side trail running off to the left. It leads to some ledgy outlooks from sea stacks with fine views over the river. Use caution here.

You now walk north well above the river, continuing along the Harraseeket Trail. The path follows the edge of the banking in and out of coves and inlets, crosses a little brook, and then turns inland and rises through groves of immense hemlocks. At the top of the rise you recross the road and plunge back into the woods on the other side. You walk east next and across a little-used fire road bordered by lowbush blueberries and then pull around to the southeast. On this inviting and quiet rib of land you are not far from the site of the Means Massacre, which took place in May 1756. Indians attacked a fortified house here, killing the master and kidnapping one of the children. Means the elder was the last white man killed by an Indian in Maine.

The trail now bears around to the east and descends to the Casco Bay Trail once again. Turn left here and, in a few moments of walking northward, you'll emerge at the trailhead and parking lot where you began this hike. The distance around this loop is less than 2 miles and can be done in a leisurely hour-and-a-half walk.

Visitors to Wolf Neck Woods will find rest rooms,

fireplaces, and picnic benches along the north and east sides of the parking area that are available for use during the park's open season.

Because thieves have occasionally burglarized cars here, do not leave valuables of any kind in your vehicle, especially when parked on the paved road outside the park entrance in the off-season.

33 · Josephine Newman Sanctuary

Location: Georgetown, Maine
Distance: 1½ miles
Walking time: 2 hours

Sometimes the attractiveness of a few, unspoiled acres so involves an individual that a lifetime connection results, a feeling bred in the bone. In more than one case, this sense of attachment has resulted in the careful preservation of some unique coastal feature and, later, public access to these special places. The Newman Sanctuary is just such a natural emblem, lodged in a coastal inlet in the diminutive island community of Georgetown.

Josephine Oliver Newman survived to the ripe old age of 90, and from the time she was a little girl until her death, she frequented the woods, fields, and ledgy shores of Georgetown Island. That experience, perhaps, inspired her to become the respected naturalist she was in later life. With Josephine Newman's death in 1968, 119 acres of unique Georgetown land, bounded on two sides by the lovely tidal waters of Robinhood Cove, passed into the hands of the Maine Audubon Society. Newman's foresight and generous gift have resulted in this exceptional peninsula being permanently secured as a natural sanctuary. Several inviting trails have been created within the preserve, and Maine Audubon now welcomes visitors from sunrise to sunset throughout the year. The preserve draws you in: its terrain varied and interesting, its foliage an attractive mix of deciduous and coniferous woodland, and, of course, its frontage on tidal Robinhood Cove quite beautiful.

The fields and shores where Josephine Newman grew up and explored lie off ME 127, 9 miles *south* of its junction with US 1 in Woolwich. Drive *south* on ME 127 and watch carefully as you pass the new post office and make a sharp bend eastward in Georgetown. Descending, cross the new bridge over the west side of Robinhood Cove. A sign by an inconspicuous side road on the *south* side of ME 127 just beyond the bridge marks the entrance to the park. The preserve road is just before the steps to Georgetown Public Library, should you have trouble finding it. This gravel entrance road is rough and sometimes wet, so head in carefully and park off to the side of the lot at the end of the road. In winter a car can be left next to the library steps; the preserve road is not plowed.

The forested terrain of the Newman Sanctuary is draped over ribs of upfolded metamorphosed rock deposited in the Devonian period more than 300 million years ago. Outcrops of rock typical of these deposits, mostly schists and quartzite, can be seen along the trails. The sanctuary plays host to many plant, bird, and animal species. Maine Audubon's booklet *Forests, Fields and Estuaries,* a guide to the preserve, lists 58 types of wildflowers, grasses, and sedges; 39 shrub species; 19 varieties of trees; 7 types of mosses and lichens; and 14 varieties of woodferns.

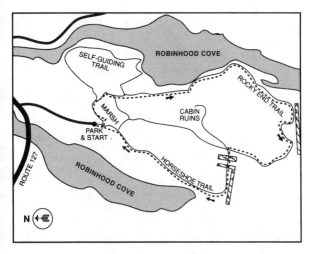

When you're ready to walk, go south from the parking area under tall, lacy white pines until you come to a signboard at the edge of the pasture. The three major trails that thread the sanctuary all depart from and return to this marker. Turn sharply around to the left and east here on the Blue Self-Guiding Trail, which you will follow to the Rocky End Trail, the route you will walk most of the way. The blue-blazed pathway drops quickly into a pretty coniferous forest and past a low stone wall. A sunken, reed-grown marsh lies off to your right. In just minutes you come to the point where the Blue Trail departs left to make a loop over to the reversing falls on Robinhood Cove. Pass this turn, keep right and continue south and southeast, looking for the red blazes that denote the Rocky End Trail. Shortly you pass another trail coming in on your right around the south end of the marsh. Continuing southward, you find yourself on the return end of the blue-blazed trail, which leads in a few more steps to the Rocky End Trail

on your right. The junction of these two trails is under a canopy of attractive mixed-growth forest, including red and white pine, red oak, white birch, red spruce, and balsam. Sometimes you can see box turtles here that have come out of the pond, perhaps to lay eggs back in the protected, sandy brush.

Turning onto the Rocky End Trail, you tramp south under lofty white pines underpinned by enormous root systems that are visible in the trail's surface for some distance. Still walking southward, you begin to descend through a grove of spindly, close-grown young balsams intermixed with red spruce. Winterberry holly, wild strawberry, dwarf sarsaparilla, and wild cherry provide ground cover. The Rocky End Trail now dips sharply to the edge of Robinhood Cove. This channel boasts stiff tidal currents with a 6- to 8-foot tidal range. If you walk here during low tide, you'll look out over mudflats extending toward the main channel. Quahogs, small macoma, and soft-shell clams live in the flats. Yellow lichens and some of the mosses common to the sanctuary blanket the ledges above the shore. Salt hay and cordgrass grow in marshy pockets along the edge of the flats.

Now you walk southeast, staying close to the water in more balsam and red spruce growth. At a giant bent pine the route begins to pull away from Robinhood Cove (just above a small nub of land that juts out into the cove) and climbs uphill sharply along a big, ledgy formation to your right. In this higher and drier ground, beech, oak, and maple supplant the evergreens that characterized the path nearer the water. Soon you arrive at a fine old stone wall that marks the southern boundary of the preserve. Go right and west here over a series of rock ribs, soon descending southwest through a stand of balsam. Trailing arbutus, bellwort, meadowsweet, hazelnut, winterberry holly, and starflower are seen at ground level in-season.

As you walk around more to the north, the trail opens up in stands of big gray birch and red oak. Still on the high ground of the sanctuary, you gradually walk downhill, coming soon to an open crossing with the Orange (Horseshoe) Trail. Bear left here, dropping down to the west through young balsams and crossing two stone walls, one of which then parallels the trail for a short distance. You come to an old tote road in a few minutes and bear right and northward again. The route now runs above and to the right of a streambed that is dry part of the year. The stream drains the upland into Robinhood Cove during spring runoff.

The deciduous woods along this stretch of trail are host to many types of bird life. Maine Audubon lists 38 bird species that live and breed in the sanctuary and another 31 that are temporarily resident during certain times of the year. Small, familiar birds such as the American goldfinch, red-winged blackbird, black-capped chickadee, and American robin are common. Larger birds are also seen, including barred owls, pileated woodpeckers, great blue herons, and snowy egrets. This walk provides an excellent opportunity to become acquainted with a variety of avian wildlife, even if you're not a birding expert. It's a good idea to carry your binoculars, and if you have room bring one of the popular bird guides, such as the *National Audubon Society Field Guide to North American Birds: Eastern Region* or Roger Tory Peterson's *A Field Guide to Birds.*

You walk northward now on the Horseshoe Trail (orange blazes) through heavy brush surrounded by groves of aspen and pine. In minutes you come to the low end of the pasture and proceed across it to the signboard where you commenced the walk. Continue northward beyond the sign a few paces to the parking area and your car.

A highly detailed description of the preserve and its unique natural features is contained in *Forests, Fields and Estuaries,* noted earlier. The publication, which also contains directions for a self-guided walk along the Blue Trail, can be obtained by sending $3.50 plus 50 cents postage to: Maine Audubon, 118 U.S. Route 1 South, Falmouth, ME 04105. The guide is especially useful to teachers and parents of young children who would like to read and learn about local ecology; it is an interesting read for the adult tramper as well.

34 · Montsweag Preserve

Location: Woolwich, Maine
Distance: 1 ¼ miles
Walking time: 1 ¼ hours

Anyone enthusiastically committed to exploring unspoiled, wooded terrain gradually recognizes that some of the most rewarding places to walk require a little detective work. In coastal New England, particularly in Maine, a number of beautiful but not-so-easy-to-spot woodlands carry you down to the shore, providing you can find them. The Montsweag Preserve offers an absorbing stroll along coastal waters, but you must sing for your supper unless you are clever enough to use this guide to lead you there, *sans* difficulty.

Though it is near several other good coastal walks in Sagadahoc County and not far from the active Bath-Brunswick area, this stroll through the Montsweag Preserve takes some detectivelike reconnoitering to find. Not that Montsweag lies in some distant, remote province. It's merely that the wooded, untrammeled nature of the place rather camouflages it to the casual eye. You need to pay attention to locate the trailhead on this walk, even though it's only minutes from US 1. The effort is well rewarded, for the loop walk within the preserve introduces the walker to the type of coastal inlet and backlands usually inaccessible because they are

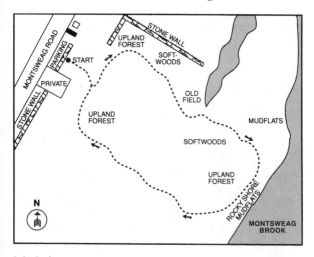

labeled private property.

Driving south from Wiscasset or north from Bath on US 1, look for Montsweag Road on the *east* side of the highway, about 0.5 mile south of the old Montsweag Farm Restaurant building in Woolwich. The road is just north of a home bakery if you are coming from Woolwich and Bath. A sign on a tree indicates the road, which runs at a sharp angle off US 1, but you will need to drive slowly not to miss it. Go *south* on Montsweag Road for 1.25 miles, watching closely for a blue-blazed tree on the *left*. It's hard to spot, and you can drive blithely on, missing the trailhead entirely. Watch for power-line pole 56–57, on which there is a small, yellowish nature preserve sign. The trailhead lies back in the woods just to the left of the pole. Get your car off the road on the shoulder as much as possible; no other parking exists.

Beginning the walk, you step through clusters of ground juniper and come at once to a hidden signboard

in a pine grove. A rough map of the preserve loop is carved here. The path will take you from this high and dry tableland, through some back marsh, and eventually along the ledgy shore of the inlet opposite Chewonki Neck. The trail tends to be brushy and grown up in places, so it is a good idea to pay attention to blazes as you walk. Carry a compass if you're one of those who doesn't have a good intuitive sense of direction. If you should lose the trail, remember that the walk to the inlet runs primarily eastward. The return, after a tramp southward along the inlet, runs mostly west and northwest back to the road.

Descend southeastward from the sign on dry ground with a stone wall to your right. White pines will give way to scrub oak as you come, in minutes, to a trail junction. Watch for two wooden arrows on a tree. You bear left here, walking to the northeast along an open path. Some trees have come down here in recent years. You pass through an old stone wall shortly and begin to rise on easy grades through a corridor of stunted white pines that frame the trail. The path next reaches a high point at the edge of a small, narrow meadow. You make an abrupt right turn here, dropping east down the right side of this open ground. A blue blaze and arrows mark the turn. The meadow is cut once in a while; the trail may be obvious or obscure, depending upon when you arrive.

At the bottom of the meadow the trail reenters the woods just west of the marsh by a big white pine to your right. Walk southeast and south here in a grove of pines, watching carefully for blazes. The trail bears left and east again in 100 yards, arriving at the edge of the marsh by a solitary pine. In this section the trail isn't well marked, and you will have to navigate a short way on your own. Keeping to the right of this pine tree, walk due east across the tail of the marsh in tall reeds. The ground may be rather wet here, depending on the season. Cordgrass and salt hay yield quickly to somewhat firmer ground, and you come to an old woods road on the other side. Walk up this sheltered road to the east, where you'll spot another blaze just in from the marsh. Continuing eastward on level terrain, you come soon to a point where the trail leaves the road and runs sharply left out onto a spit of land. A tidal inlet lies below to the left. Beech, oak, and pine are replaced by hemlock and balsam as the trail skirts lichen-covered granite where there are fine views northward.

Running northeast, east, and eventually south, the path follows the water's edge. Across the inlet, the docks of the Chewonki Foundation become visible on Chewonki Neck. The channel runs north and south, its calm interrupted only by an occasional boat and the effect of the tides.

Walk south now, paralleling the stream in groves of beech. The trail soon begins to rise in stands of fir and hemlock, passing an exposed ledge to the right. You can see well down Montsweag Brook toward some islets that lie off to the south. Open ledge along the brook provides a number of places to sit, rest, and perhaps eat lunch. At low tide, mudflats along the bank may be worth cautious exploration.

Continuing south, watch very carefully for a three-trunked oak where the trail abruptly turns right and away from the brook. There are arrows on a tree here, indicating the turn. If you come to a stone wall, you've walked too far; backtrack and watch for the trail on your left. Follow the blazes southwestward on what may have been another woods road, passing over a series of granite ribs. You soon descend into a boggy area by a boulder pile that was probably part of an old foundation. Passing through this boggy slump, the trail now marches west through a brushy area to a grove of great white pines. To the left is another low, wet area that channels runoff to Montsweag Brook.

As you walk inland, the trail dips briefly and then climbs gradually to the west and northwest. Passing a side trail that runs west toward a house, the route pulls around to the north, bringing you to the junction marked by arrows noted earlier. Bear left at this junction, walking the feeder trail up through the brush to the road.

The 1 1/4-mile Montsweag Loop can be walked easily in an hour and a half. Allow more time for shoreline exploration and picnicking.

35 · Fernald's Neck

Location: Camden, Maine
Distance: 1¼ miles
Walking time: 1½ hours

Fernald's Neck is one of the prettiest accessible hemlock forests on the Maine coast, a perfect tramping ground for hikers, bird-watchers, or anyone interested in the plant and animal life of coastal Maine. This irregular, north–south peninsula in Megunticook Lake contains more than 300 acres of forest and bog with over 18,000 feet of unspoiled shoreline. The Nature Conservancy owns and protects a number of rare properties in the Maine coastal zone, but Fernald's Neck, in Camden and Lincolnville, has to be one of the most attractive of the lot.

This broad preserve was formerly pasture, cultivated farmland, and woodlot, but in recent years it has reverted to its natural state. Named for Nathaniel Fernald and his heirs, who first settled here in 1806, the neck nearly fell to the developers in the late 1960s. Aggressive action by local citizens resulted in purchase of the land and its subsequent donation to The Nature Conservancy, under whose care it will remain forever wild.

Visitors to the neck should drive *west* on ME 52 from US 1 in Camden center. The road follows the long expanse of Megunticook Lake toward Lincolnville.

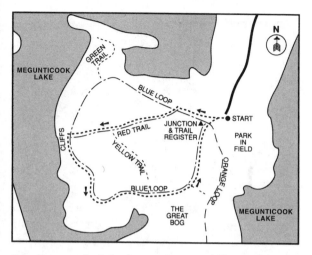

Coming to a fork in the road at Young's Corner, stay *left* on ME 52, round a curve, and watch for a side road on the *left* marked F.R. 50. You bear *left* and southwest off the pavement, driving in on Fire Road 50 past several cottages on the northeast shore of Megunticook. At a Nature Conservancy sign on a tree, go *left* on a gravel road. This track leads you south to a farmhouse that you skirt to the right, entering an open pasture. (If you arrive during mud season, you may want to leave your car by the sign and walk the last stretch to this field.) Park your car in the grassy lot behind the farmhouse.

This walk begins amid beautiful views northeast to Maiden Cliff on the back side of Mount Megunticook. Hike south and southwest on a path downhill through the field and look for a break in the stone wall where the path enters the woods. The walk continues south-west in a densely grown tunnel of balsam and hemlock. Off to the left, occasional breaks in the trees allow you to see Megunticook Lake. Low ground makes for wet

walking briefly, and then you rise southward to a fine grove of stately hemlocks. Passing through a stone wall, you arrive at a trail junction with a trail register and signboard. In the brush to the left, an old logging ramp molders in the shade. At the register box you will usually find copies of the *Fernald's Neck Preserve Guide*. When you sign the register, be sure the box is closed and latched against the weather.

Two loops depart from this clearing. One (the Orange Loop) runs south to the central bulge in the neck. We'll take the Blue and Red Trails, which cover a generous section of the northern area of the preserve. From the register, walk right and west on the Blue Loop Trail. The path here arches westward under more big hemlocks, passing the Blue Loop return and coming shortly to the Red Trail on your left. Turn left and southwest here, rising slowly through young growth that crowds the trail. This stretch has a travel-brochure quality to it, the path meandering under tier after tier of perfectly manicured hemlocks rising in a great overhead canopy. The Yellow Trail, a link, comes in on the left. You pass several trees punctured by pileated woodpeckers, which raid the bark for insect larvae. A clutch of large boulders, deposited here as glacial erratics, is approached soon, as is a stagnant little tarn off to the left. You come then to the ledges and scramble back onto the Blue Trail, turning left and south. Ground juniper, white and red pine, and the ubiquitous hemlock cover the ledges as you climb slightly. Fallen logs and thick beds of lime-green lichen lie scattered about. Before long you emerge on a high, open ledge with excellent views over the west arm of Megunticook Lake. The prospect over some of the surrounding mountains to the south appeals as well. Ducks and seabirds that come inland to visit the lake may be seen paddling about below the ledges. This lookout makes about the best lunch and rest stop, and spending some time here is recommended.

The trail now descends into the woods over several ledgy ribs and then, turning sharply east through white pine and fine hemlock groves, runs along the preserve boundary. Farther eastward you soon approach what is called the Great Bog, a swampy area home to many plant and avian species. The *Fernald's Neck Preserve Guide* notes: "The bog is surrounded by an array of aquatic plants such as pipewort, arrowhead, burreed, pondweeds and bulrushes. Much of the bog is covered with leatherleaf, sweet gale, rhodora and other shrubs that tolerate wet, acid soils. Sphagnum moss forms the bog surface, supporting pitcher plants, rose pogonia, blue flag iris and a variety of ferns, sedges, grasses and rushes. Wood ducks, red-winged blackbirds, Canada geese, and black ducks nest or visit."

Passing through a range of boulders and silver birch, the path dips and then rises gradually eastward past the Yellow Trail as it appears to the left. The walk now pulls around to the north after passing still another section of the Yellow Trail on the right. The way gets dampish here; sphagnum and haircap mosses flourish on the often unstable, waterlogged ground. The shelf fungus *Ganoderma tsuga* grows avidly on old fallen hemlocks. Shortly you arrive at a junction where you keep right and north to the register box.

From the register clearing, retrace your steps northeastward toward the pasture. If you watch carefully, you will find a narrow, unmarked path on your right before you come to the border of the field. You may want to take a moment to follow this rough trail a short distance eastward to where it offers attractive waterside views down Megunticook. Once back on the main path, continue northeast and north up through the pasture to your starting point. Allow at least an hour and a half for this loop around the upper half of the preserve.

36 • Mount Megunticook

Location: Camden, Maine
Distance: 2 to 7 miles (depending on route selected)
Walking time: 2 to 5 hours

Mount Megunticook is situated centrally in the nine low peaks known as the Camden Hills, all of which ring the pretty coastal Maine town that Edna St. Vincent Millay made famous as the place "where the mountains come down to the sea." Most who visit Camden want to explore its village center and harborfront, bustling with tourists and the yachting set in the warm months, much quieter in winter. Sooner or later the visitor turns to the hills as being more interesting than gift shops and eateries, and Megunticook welcomes, a sizable presence northwest of the village.

This walk scribes a loop over the highest of the Camden Hills, delivering the kind of broad, seaward views that spoil you for cities forever. A couple of hours of pleasant walking will take you up Megunticook's northeast slope, on to Ocean Lookout, and steeply down the mountain's southeast ledges to your starting point at Camden Hills State Park. The Megunticook loop makes a fine three-season walk and can be done even in winter by those who are properly equipped. In high summer this walk is best done on weekdays, when the path is unlikely to be crowded, making your progress to the summit refreshing and solitary.

In midcoast Maine drive *north* on US 1 from Camden center, bearing *left* into Camden Hills State Park about 2.75 miles from town. Camping sites are available here for those who arrive early. A parking lot for day hikers lies under the trees to the left of the gatehouse. A modest fee for day use is paid at the gatehouse.

Park staff can provide you with a free map of the trail network. The Appalachian Mountain Club's Camden Hills map is for sale in some local stores. (See also the author's *50 Hikes in Coastal and Southern Maine*, Backcountry Publications, and *Walking the Maine Coast*, Down East Books, both available in local stores, for further walks in the Camden region.)

The route runs west along the park road through the campground, coming shortly to a gravel way marked MEGUNTICOOK TRAIL. This trail shortly crosses a footbridge and pulls to the northwest. Walking through open stands of beech and ash, the trail slabs quickly uphill twice to the southwest, levels off, and then gradually runs northwest again on easy grades. The path follows an old tote road for some distance.

Again you walk westerly and southwesterly as the trail begins a progression of steeper pitches over a series of granite ribs. A brook, more often than not dry, is passed. Deciduous foliage slowly gives way to groves of conifers. Red spruce, balsam, and some white pine are seen. Climbing through several more brisk rises, the trail pulls nearly south and eases up in grassy groves of red oak. Walking past a clearing with views oceanward, you soon come to Ocean Lookout.

Before you are some of the most splendid views of

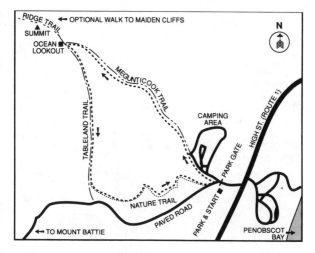

midcoast Maine. To the immediate southeast is the summit of nearby Mount Battie, with its distinctive stone tower. Camden perches below on its fine harbor. Well out to sea are the north–south islands of North Haven and Vinalhaven, and beyond, the whaleback shape of Isle au Haut. Ragged and Bald Mountains form the range to the southwest. On a clear day you can view the coast southward for 30 or 40 miles.

The actual summit of Megunticook will be found a short way uphill and inland, but it is wooded. If you have the time, this walk northwest along the ridge trail to Maiden Cliff will reward your effort with fine views from the cliffs over Megunticook Lake and the countryside to the west. The distance to Maiden Cliff is about 2½ miles one-way and requires around three hours round trip. This side trip is highly recommended if you want to convert a short ramble into a more demanding walk that will occupy the better part of a day. The periodic views are superb.

Whether you continue inland and return or head down directly from Ocean Lookout, you will take the Tablelands Trail off the ledges to the southeast. This path winds down and under the ledges, eventually working its way southwest and south to the oak- and beech-shaded tableland between Megunticook and Mount Battie. You go past the Carriage Trail on the right shortly, then continue south to the Nature Trail about ¾ mile below Ocean Lookout.

Bear left and east on the Nature Trail, which dips into some low, wet ground briefly and then climbs a ledgy rib. More spruce and pine line the path, which next descends northeast and north into beech forest. Continuing northeasterly, the trail loses altitude gradually, crosses a couple of small, seasonal brooks, and works its way gradually rightward at a trail junction to a new hikers' parking area on the Mount Battie auto road. From this parking lot walk downward, left and northeast, along the auto road back to the point where you left your car at the main gate. A short walk past the gatehouse below will bring you back to the hikers' parking area where you started.

This loop can be walked in two hours, but that would be needlessly rushing it. Allow for at least an additional half hour or hour at Ocean Lookout, and add another three hours if you walk to Maiden Cliff and return before descending.

37 · Crockett Cove Woods

Location: Stonington, Maine
Distance: 1½ miles
Walking time: 1¼ hours

In 1975 Stonington artist and architect Emily Muir generously donated 100 acres of prime coastal woodland just back of Crockett Cove to The Nature Conservancy. The Conservancy's guide to Crockett Cove Woods calls this exceptional acreage a coastal fog forest, as the land is perfectly placed to capture the wind and wet air off Penobscot Bay. Not surprisingly, this island position guarantees that Crockett Cove Woods will harbor a unique range of vegetation and wildlife in its moist, cool environs. If you are usually a fair-weather hiker, you might want to consider the Conservancy's advice to walk this ground on a foggy (or dirty) day, when its wild flora take on a brilliant luminescence in the damp coastal air. Of course, walking here on a fine, sunny spring or summer day does no harm either.

Crockett Cove hides on the west side of attractive Deer Isle. Hunkered down in the sea to the south of Eggemoggin Reach, Deer Isle is a large landmass at the end of the Blue Hill Peninsula. It has the virtue of being well off the beaten path, down pleasant back roads dotted with small fishing communities not yet spoiled by the arrival of progress. Though an island in fact, Deer

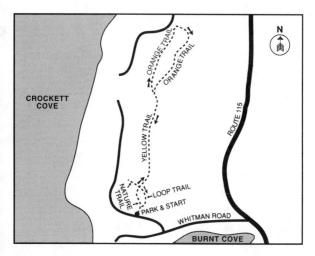

Isle can be reached conveniently via a pretty suspension bridge to the mainland. Deer Isle is home to the Haystack School, one of the country's premier seasonal craft schools. Artists, artisans, lobstermen, and fishermen live side by side here. It is an unhurried place of considerable beauty, both in the island's few villages and its wild areas.

To reach Deer Isle, drive *south* from US 1 in midcoast Orland on ME 15. In Deer Isle township bear *right* and *south* on an unnumbered road to Sunset. Pass Perez Cross Road and Sunset Cross Road as you descend southward. Driving through Sunset, watch for Whitman Road on the *right* about 2.5 miles south of the Sunset post office. (If you arrive at this point from the direction of Stonington village, Whitman Road will be on your left approximately 2 miles north of town.) Turn *right* and go west on Whitman Road along the edge of scenic Burnt Cove. Bear right on a side road marked FL 88, pass a barrier, and enter the woods. The trailhead and a small parking area lie just around a bend to the *right*. Sign in at the trail register.

Four paths meander around Crockett Cove Woods. Those walking with youngsters may want to try the Nature Trail first. This short walk has 19 guideposts keyed to a self-guiding nature map, copies of which are usually available in the register box. Making this short, easy introductory walk will acquaint you with the bird and animal life, ground cover, and forest growth typical of the preserve.

At the north end of the short nature walk, turn around and retrace your steps briefly, then turn left and walk north through the center of the preserve on the yellow-blazed Hiking Trail or, simply, Yellow Trail. This solitary route runs through a cedar forest and mixed deciduous and coniferous woods, crossing and recrossing a small brook several times. You'll shortly reach tall, robust stands of spruce, and a trail junction not far beyond.

By the time you've walked this far, you will have noticed the lush, prolific understory growth that is typical of the preserve. Bracken fern, Indian pipe, withe rod, creeping snowberry, cinnamon fern, pitcher plants, bunchberry, mountain holly, sheep laurel, and large and small cranberry flourish in this terrain.

Red and white spruce both thrive on the moist air and wet, acidic soil. The red is characterized by its bright green needles and smallish, golden brown cones. White spruce has coarser, blue-green needles and larger cones. Each year people buy white spruce Christmas trees and later wish they hadn't. This tree has also been labeled skunk spruce or cat spruce by those who know the woods. When a white spruce has languished in some-

one's warm living room for a few days, a marvelously powerful, skunklike odor begins to permeate the air. People so afflicted often throw the tree, lights and all, out on the front lawn in a fit of pique. White spruce are better left in the woods.

Striped and red maple, tamarack, black alder, and cedar line the trail now, and the observant naturalist will discover whorled wood aster, red trillium, baneberry, round-leaved sundew, goldthread, twinflower, and bluebead lily. Most of these species are described in the brochure that guides the nature walk.

You may go either way at the junction noted above. (The Orange Trail circles through the middle third of the preserve, bringing you back to this junction.) Walking north to the top of this loop, you come to another entrance to the woods. Passing this northern entrance, continue around the Orange Trail circuit, watching for some of the wildlife common to the place. Red squirrels, the ubiquitous striped skunk, snowshoe hares, weasels, deer mice, white-tailed deer, masked shrews, and raccoons reside here.

Shortly, the orange-blazed loop returns you to the Yellow (Hiking) Trail, where you retrace your steps outward to the southern end of the park. Approaching your starting point, follow the Loop Trail leftward as it makes an arc through strikingly beautiful coniferous forest, and then brings you out to the signboard where you commenced the walk. This circuit from the south to the north gate and back, with a little time spent on the Nature Trail by way of introduction, can be completed in a comfortable hour and a half to two hours.

Waterproof hiking shoes or boots will add to your comfort on this walk over what is frequently low ground. Please stay on the trails, and do not disturb plants, shrubs, or flowers as you walk.

38 · Blagden Preserve, Indian Point

Location: Mount Desert Island, Maine
Distance: 2⅓ miles
Walking time: 2 hours

The Blagden Preserve is a serene, densely wooded natural reservation at Mount Desert Island's western limits on Indian Point. Donated to The Nature Conservancy in 1968 by Donald and Zelina Blagden, this quiet waterfront preserve is typical of the wooded parts of Mount Desert that escaped the tragic Bar Harbor fires of 1947.

Geographically, Indian Point forms an unspoiled, narrow thumb of land that presses out into Western Bay at the tidal northwestern corner of Mount Desert Island, just southwest of Town Hill. In the center of the point rests that 110-acre strip of land known as the Blagden Preserve. Walking these inviting woods you get a sense of Mount Desert as it once was, thickly forested in conifers and old hardwoods, surrounded by rich, varied understory growth. A unique walk of nearly 2½ miles can be made within the preserve boundaries, from road to ocean and back; if you've picked the right day, you may find seals taking their leisure on the rocky shores of Western Bay.

To reach Indian Point, drive onto Mount Desert Island from Trenton on ME 3. Cross Mount Desert Narrows and, once you're past the visitors information center at Thompson's Island, you come to a Y in the road by a filling station–convenience store. Keep *right* here and follow ME 102/198 *south* toward Somesville. About 2 miles from the Y, turn *right* off ME 102 onto Indian Point Road. Follow this road for 1.75 miles to the preserve entrance on your *right*. You'll find a grassy parking space just inside on the *right*.

Register at the caretaker's cottage on arrival. From the parking area, walk northward along the Rockwall Trail, which follows a stone wall behind the cottage, makes a U-turn, and comes out to the preserve road north of the cottage. Here you cross the road and walk west on the Big Woods Trail. Scattered birches, hemlock, and red spruce provide a shady canopy over level, root-knotted ground. The moist coastal air feeds beard lichens, which grow like wispy green whiskers on surrounding trees.

You pull northwest and northward among tall hemlock and spruce, walking on boggy, moss-rich ground. The brilliant lacy green of haircap and sphagnum mosses colors the borders of the path. The pungent scent of dry balsam emanates from a clump of blowdown. Views ahead of the bay, partially obscured by brush, open up briefly as you move into white pine growth and arrive shortly at a little-used gravel road.

Bear left just a few yards on this road and then immediately turn right back into the woods, picking up the trail again in low, wet ground where there are a series of log platforms on which to walk. You pass through more blowdowns in this thickly forested sec-

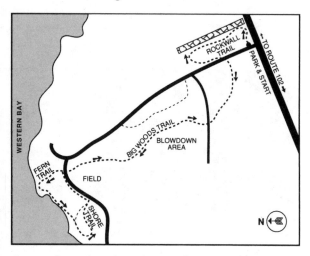

tion and reach a junction with a connecting trail momentarily. Stay left here and continue walking north and northwest, heading downhill in more open woods and soon passing a second connector trail on the right. (These connectors link with the Grass and Moss Trail and, eventually, the preserve road.) Continue straight on and through a rough stand of red cedars. Wet ground occurs again as you pass more spruce and arrive at a clearing. Alder, cedar, and hackmatack grow beside the path as it becomes a grassy, open road, which you now walk to an orchard and the preserve road. By this stage you have lost some altitude and are at the low end of the point, only a little above the shore.

Cross the preserve road northwestward and, staying to the left of a fence, walk toward Western Bay. You descend along this short path (known as the Fern Trail) to the ledges. Excellent views up and down Western Bay are before you when you emerge from the woods. Ellsworth schist, the striped ledge that lies all about, is

aged stuff, laid down here at least 450 million years ago. The shoreline is littered with boulders deposited by glacial movement from points inland.

A path, slightly inland, goes southwest through the woods a few yards to a beach. This stretch provides some interesting turf for beachcombers and more good water-level outlooks over Western Bay. At the end of the beach a seal haul-out, really some flat rocks, lies just offshore. You may find harbor seals basking above the tide in spring and summer. When you have had your fill of the shore, follow the Shore Trail back to the paved road. (Please stay off private property around the western waterfront boundary of the preserve.)

On the return, you can vary the route if you wish. Probably the most direct way back to the caretaker's house is simply walking the paved road southeastward for a brisk, uphill tramp of about a mile. A second alternative is to retrace your steps on the Big Woods Trail. Or you can walk part of the way back on the road, cutting right into the woods at the halfway point on the Grass and Moss Trail. This path loops through some pretty woods, curving back to the road just above the caretaker's place.

Blagden Preserve remains open throughout the year, but winter visitors would do well to call ahead to ask whether trails are open. Ring up the caretaker at (207) 288-4838. Bird-watchers will find at the trail register a list of species typically seen in the preserve.

39 · Eagle Cliffs and Saint Sauveur Mountain

Location: Acadia National Park, Mount
  Desert Island, Maine
Distance: 2½ miles
Walking time: 2 hours

Mount Desert Island is an accidental signpost in
early American history. The earliest explorations
of the Atlantic coast in the New World touched shore
here. The island, in fact, takes its name from the record-
ed remarks of early French explorers who referred to its
bare, mountainous profile as "les Isles du Monts
Deserts." Today Mount Desert Island's great horseshoe-
shaped landmass enfolds Acadia National Park, and its
dozens of hiking trails offer spectacular views of the
open Atlantic.

Saint Sauveur Mountain is one of those very pictur-
esque low summits that form the castellated western
border of Somes Sound, a fjordlike inlet that more or
less divides Mount Desert Island right up the middle.
The hill takes its name from the short-lived French settlement thrown up here by the Jesuits in 1613. The
French settlers were soon captured and their little
colony broken up by the crew of the aggressive British
frigate *Treasurer*. The name Saint Sauveur has stuck,

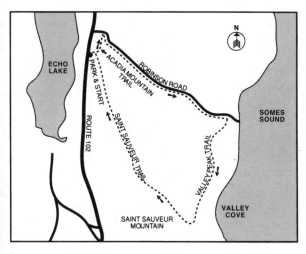

however, and the low mountain (just under 700 feet in altitude) that bears it merits your attention, for some of the most dramatic views seen in Acadia National Park are found on this pleasant loop. That this walk rises on the west side of Mount Desert near Echo Lake, far from the tourist traps of Bar Harbor, makes it all the more desirable.

Entering Mount Desert from Trenton on ME 3, bear *right* after you pass the Thompson Island Information Center and go *south* on ME 102/198 through Town Hill and Somesville toward Southwest Harbor. Three miles south of Somesville on ME 102, watch for a parking area on the *west* side of the road above Echo Lake. You'll see the trailhead opposite. Paths also run down through the woods from this lot to the east shore of Echo Lake, where swimming is possible.

Cross ME 102 carefully and head up the steps by the Acadia Mountain Trail into the woods. You rise quickly from the road through jack pines, then lowbush blueberries, and over pink granite ledge to the southeast. The terrain is open for a short distance, and then you reenter thick woods grown up in white pine, red pine, and white spruce. Lichens spot the ledges. A big boulder is passed on the left as more birches appear, and you arrive soon at a trail junction where the Saint Sauveur Trail goes to the right. You will return to this point later, descending via this other trail.

For now, keep left and north through a depression grown dense with rhodora. After climbing again over several bars of ledge, you emerge on gravel Robinson Road. Bear right and southeast on this National Park Service right-of-way, which gradually descends via pretty woodlands toward the sound. Pass an attractive grove of eastern red cedar in $1/2$ mile, then walk through a field, watching for the north end of the Valley Peak Trail at a junction just before Man O' War Brook. (If you reach the shore or the route up Acadia Mountain, you've gone too far.)

The real work of the hike begins here as you go right and southward up Valley Peak Trail toward Eagle Cliffs. You will gain 500 to 600 feet of elevation in the $1/2$ mile between here and the open cliffs above. The walk upward changes from closely wooded ground to more open terrain as the path moves steadily to the southwest. Views open up to the east over Somes Sound as you gain elevation. The rocky mass of Acadia Mountain is over your shoulder as the route clambers up the rough precipice. Moving along a series of ledges (watch your footing carefully), you arrive ultimately at the Eagle Cliffs site well above Valley Cove and the great north–south pocket of Somes Sound.

Saint Sauveur shares this spectacular view of the

sound and the island-dotted ocean with its nearby neighbors, Flying and Acadia Mountains. I could drum up a lot of superlatives to describe the view here, but it's enough to merely note that this prospect has few equals elsewhere on the island. Just sitting and watching the summer water traffic under sail below can be fascinating. Some of the biggest sailing yachts on the eastern seaboard find their way to anchorage in Somes Sound in the course of the warm months, and all that majestic traffic can be observed from Eagle Cliffs as if by command performance. Norumbega, Penobscot, Pemetic, and Cadillac Mountains, one behind the other, are across the sound in a line to the northeast.

Directly below lies Valley Cove, a pretty inlet, and just south of the cove is Flying Mountain. At the south end of the sound, Greening Island, Sutton Island, Great Cranberry, Little Cranberry, and Baker Islands roll southeastward on the Atlantic. The town across the sound is Northeast Harbor; to the south lies Southwest

Harbor. Find a good spot on the top of the cliffs to sit and observe for a while.

To continue the loop, walk west and northwest through close-grown scrub toward Saint Sauveur's true summit. (*Don't* head left and downward toward Valley Peak.) A few hundred yards westward you wind your way to a clearing. Turn right here and you come to Saint Sauveur's wooded top, a ledgy, flat area open only to the northeast. The walk proceeds mainly northward now, over a stretch of root-covered ground, descending slowly to a junction with the Ledge Trail, which comes in on the left after its ascent from ME 102. Pass this side trail and continue to the northwest and west, winding through a grove of eastern red cedar. The route drops down over some ledge and goes north again through red spruce for a way, and then pulls to the northwest and another junction by some ledge and boulders.

You continue rightward to the north again as the trail moves down over a series of knobs grown over by wind-blown jack pines. Fine views over the narrow, north–south finger of water that is Echo Lake are before you for most of the descent over this ledgy, attractive terrain. Aspens, red maples, and a wind-toppled old pine line the path as you arrive at a junction with the Acadia Trail. This is the junction you tramped through early in the walk. Go left and west for the short walk out to the road and parking area.

This loop can be hiked in all seasons, but good footwear and caution should be priorities when the ledges are wet or icy. In normal summer conditions, the Saint Sauveur loop can be walked in two hours.

40·Dorr Mountain and Cadillac Mountain

Location: Acadia National Park, Mount Desert Island, Maine
Distance: 3½ miles
Walking time: 3 hours

In 1604 the adventurous French explorer Samuel de Champlain discovered Mount Desert Island along Maine's northern coast. Maine's only national park today occupies a good part of the island and provides some of the most outstanding hill walking on the New England shore. Acadia National Park currently serves walkers with 120 miles of trails in a mountainous setting of more than 30,000 acres. Most of the popular walks in Acadia take the walker near the shore, along or over some of the fine ponds, lakes, or sounds on the island, or upward on ledgy trails that deliver vast panoramic views of the open Atlantic. Walking here is unforgettable.

Mount Desert is reached by driving *east* on ME 3 from Ellsworth. Crossing from the mainland to the island at Trenton, drive ME 3 farther *eastward*, watching for the Acadia National Park Information Center in the direction of Bar Harbor. Detailed maps of the park, the island, and connecting roads can be obtained at the visitors center. Guided nature walks are also scheduled here periodically. Inquire for additional information on bicycling, snowshoeing, and cross-country skiing in the park.

When planning walks in Acadia, visitors should consult the park map carefully. Many park sites are accessible by both state roads and the park service road. *Be aware that once you are on the park service road, you must proceed around Acadia, mainly in one direction.* An Acadia park road pass costs $5.00 and is valid for one week. If you want to day-hike in the park, you can reach most of the hills in Acadia (including those walks described here) from ME 3, ME 198, or ME 102 instead, thus saving yourself a burdensome toll. In recent summers the park has successfully operated a shuttle bus that links major hiking destinations.

In high summer Acadia is increasingly crowded, and some island roads are busy with tourists who seem to believe that nature is best examined only from the front seat of a car. The state roads appear to be less frequented and more tranquil, particularly on Mount Desert's west side. Really, the best times to visit and walk on Mount Desert are the months of April, May, September, October, and November, when you can walk in peace and escape the summer hordes entirely. Acadia remains beautiful and unspoiled in the winter as well.

The walk up Dorr and Cadillac Mountains will introduce the tramper to two major peaks and some of the best views in Acadia. Dorr Mountain, named for George B. Dorr, one of several benefactors who worked diligently for the establishment of this national park, is the third highest mountain on the island and your first objective on this walk. From Bar Harbor, take ME 3

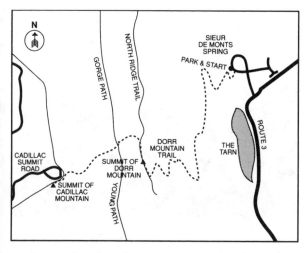

south toward Seal Harbor. Not much more than a mile south of town, bear *right* at signs for Sieur de Monts Spring. Turn in here and park by the Abbe Museum and the nature center, both of which provide interesting information on the natural and human history of the island.

From the nature center, walk toward the Spring-house. Look for a stone with the words SWEET WATERS on it. You go right here on a paved walkway that soon becomes gravel. Signs indicate the Dorr Mountain Trail, which is your route. You shortly turn northwesterly and then south, rising quickly through a series of switch-backs in young hardwoods. The trail continues south over a collection of stone steps. About ½ mile above the spring, the East Slope Trail comes in on your left, rising straight up from the north shore of the Tarn. Pass this trail and continue the climb to the south. At this point the path rises above the vegetation of the notch, and good views begin to open up north and south, and over

Huguenot Head and Champlain Mountain to the east.

The trail soon passes the Dorr Mountain Ladder Trail on the left at just over a mile from your starting point. You now turn more northwest and west, climbing briskly upward through a series of bends. The route emerges in minutes on the open summit of Dorr. Directly ahead to the west lies the great whaleback of Cadillac Mountain, Acadia's highest peak. The mountain's long spine of bare, orange-pink granite forms a brilliant plane, with the summit at the right. North of Dorr and considerably lower, you will see little Kebo Mountain, and beyond it the broad expanse of Frenchman Bay off Bar Harbor.

More work awaits, for you must now descend to the ravine between Dorr and Cadillac before scaling the main peak. From Dorr summit, walk along the North Ridge Trail briefly, turning left and west to descend on the Notch Trail in a few minutes. Here you make a fairly steep scramble down into the Otter Creek drainage area. Heading down, you reach the Gorge Path and the

Murray Young Path in ⅓ mile. Continue west and southwest, climbing on the Gorge Path to Cadillac's summit. The rise here will have you panting, but the distance isn't far. You can cover the terrain between the spring and Dorr in about an hour and a quarter, and between Dorr and Cadillac in an additional 45 minutes.

If there was any doubt about the slog up these two mountains being worth it, that doubt disappears once on the bald, open summit grounds of Cadillac. Views here include those seen from Dorr, only now the entire expanse of Mount Desert opens up in nearly all directions. The raft of islands that create the bar in Bar Harbor is fully visible. Bar Island, Sheep Porcupine, Bald Porcupine, Burnt Porcupine, and Long Porcupine Islands are the five small islands of the bar just offshore. Over Champlain you see lower Frenchman Bay and, far across the channel, Schoodic Point and Schoodic Head. Around to the southwest you'll spot Pemetic and Penobscot Mountains. Beautiful Eagle Lake lies to the northwest. Great and Little Cranberry are the two larger islands well off to the south over Seal Harbor. Way to the northeast, on the mainland, Schoodic Mountain, a good hike in itself, rises from the flat plain.

The return to Sieur de Monts will exact some further effort, as you now retrace the route of the ascent over to Dorr and then down to the road on the same trails. Including exploration of Cadillac's broad summit, the round trip takes in nearly 4 miles of fairly strenuous walking. Use caution should you descend in wet weather: Exposed rock can become slippery. The walk to Cadillac and back can be done in about four hours. Allow additional time if you plan to rest, explore, and have lunch on Cadillac's summit.

For many other walks in Acadia see the author's *50 Hikes in Coastal and Southern Maine* (Backcountry Publications) and *Walking the Maine Coast* (Down East Books).

41 · Ship Harbor Nature Trail

Location: Acadia National Park, Mount
  Desert Island, Maine
Distance: 1 mile
Walking time: 1¼ hours

Here is an easy, water-level walk near the southern-most point of Mount Desert Island above Bass Harbor Head on the back road from Southwest Harbor. If you like to stroll alone by the shore, or if you want to hike over forgiving ground where children can make their way easily, Ship Harbor beckons.

Away from it all in the quietest corner of Mount Desert Island, the Ship Harbor Nature Trail does indeed make a rewarding, leisurely walk for solitaries and families. The paths here aren't heavily frequented, and except between July 4 and Labor Day, you may well cover the circuit without seeing anyone. Because this stretch of shore reposes about as far away from the bright lights and summer congestion of Bar Harbor as you can get while still being in Acadia, its a pleasure to visit regardless of season.

The Ship Harbor Nature Trail has been set up as a self-guiding nature walk along the banks of a picture-perfect little harbor and channel. Trail markers along the route are keyed to a pamphlet available at Acadia National Park headquarters or in a box by the trailhead.

The route described here roughly duplicates that explained in the trail brochure.

To get to Ship Harbor, drive to Southwest Harbor on Mount Desert Island. Take ME 102A *left* just south of town at its junction with ME 102. Continue *east* and *south* through spectacular, eye-catching coastal terrain and across a natural seawall. Four and a quarter miles south of the junction, look for a paved parking area on the *left*. You can leave your car here near the trailhead by a big sign.

The nature path at Ship Harbor describes a figure-eight through the woods. You set out southeastward through a little hollow bordered by spruce and alder. You are to the left of the harbor here, but very close to the shore. Raspberry bushes grow wild farther on, while lichens droop like beards from the limbs of weatherworn old spruce trees. In a couple of minutes you come to a junction, where you bear left over wet ground by a pair of gray birches.

Continuing generally southeastward, the path runs down a corridor of attractive tall spruce. You pass a low, boggy depression on the left as the route pulls more to the south. Bunchberry, club moss, and a variety of lichens thickly carpet the ground adjacent to the trail. Rising over an open, ledgy hummock, the trail bends to the southwest and drops to a lovely grove by the water's edge. The views here are out to the broadened channel at the mouth of Ship Harbor. This excellent spot for berthing a ship is, as you can now see, well inland from the open ocean. In this grove, you are at the crux of the figure-eight.

You now continue up the *left* side of the figure-eight by finding a marker post and keeping *left*. The route

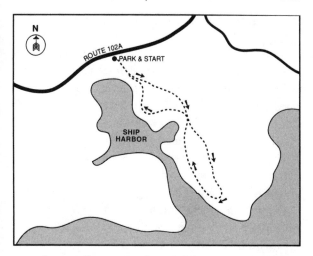

now rises easily eastward out of the grove. Gradually you work your way out from under the evergreen canopy, emerging into more open, ledgy terrain. If you are observant, you'll notice that some of this weathered ledge is marked by a series of striations. This effect, caused by the abrasive scouring of glacial movement, can be found in many places on Mount Desert. Glacial ice retreated inland as it melted back more than eleven thousand years ago.

From here to the point, tamarack (hackmatack or eastern larch) grow abundantly. Tamarack boasts clusters of bright, blue-green needles that grow in little clusters, and reddish brown, upright cones. If you walk along here in autumn, you'll find the tamaracks' needles have gone golden prior to being shed. This tree, though a conifer and a member of the pine family, is not a true evergreen, and winter finds it rather bare or still carrying some of its now dead needles. Past this stand of trees you walk through clumps of ground juniper and white spruce and emerge at the high end of the figure-eight.

From these ledges you have splendid views over open ocean. Around to the northeast are Great Cranberry Island, and farther out, Baker Island. Great Gott Island may be visible southward. Ledge and boulder border the sea and invite exploration *if the sea is calm.* Rockweed and Irish moss are visible, and barnacles cling to the rocks just below the high-tide line. Coastal rocks may be slippery, and parents should supervise youngsters carefully here.

More than three hundred species of birds come to Mount Desert's shores. One hundred twenty-two of these species breed on the island. You are likely to see several types of aquatic birds out here on the point and above the channel on the return. Remember, if you explore the rocks and ledges, *this terrain is slippery.* In stiff weather and heavy tides, these places can be dangerous.

The walk back follows the channel generally northwestward next toward Ship Harbor. You walk along the north side of the channel above the rocks. The trail gets rough in several places, and you need to watch your footing. Below are ledges of the attractive pink granite common to Mount Desert. Shortly, the trail pulls around to the right and away from the channel. You arrive at the grove you passed through earlier.

Look *left* along the shore for where the path leaves the grove and resumes its direction beside the channel and harbor. Following the shore, you continue northwest over root-crossed, stony ground. Occasional views back along the channel open up as you walk through ground juniper and balsam to a rocky hump that provides an excellent outlook to the inner harbor. Many aquatic birds gather here, and bringing along a set of binoculars to observe bird life is a good idea. Next the trail dips through a blowdown area and rises by some large birches, arriving again at the junction encountered on the outward leg. Go left and north now, coming to the parking area in a few minutes.

You can hike the Ship Harbor Trail in an hour and a quarter without hurrying. Points of natural interest along the trail—the rocks, the open sea, and the tranquil little harbor—are all worth taking extra time to inspect in a leisurely way.

42 • Schoodic Head

Location: Acadia National Park, Winter
  Harbor, Maine
Distance: 2¾ to 3⅔ miles (depending
  on route selected)
Walking time: 2 to 2½ hours

Acadia National Park lands occupy not only Mount
Desert Island, but also Isle au Haut and the
Schoodic Peninsula. On the peninsula section of Acadia, Schoodic Head, a lovely, wooded, granite mountain, rises at the southern tip below the towns of Winter Harbor and Birch Harbor. Those who walk here will
find the coastline every bit as stunning as on Mount
Desert, with dozens of rocky tidal inlets bordered by
dense evergreen forestlands. Even at the height of summer, the Schoodic Peninsula doesn't attract the crowds
because it lies well south of US 1 and its attendant rush.
This is a remarkably quiet, remote corner of Acadia
National Park that motorized tourism largely misses.
And here, on the less traveled east side of Frenchman
Bay, weekend walkers will find an enjoyable hill walk in
a natural upland with top-notch ocean views.

To walk Schoodic Head, leave US 1 on the eastern
Maine coast and drive *south* on ME 186 from West
Gouldsboro. Follow the signs to Winter Harbor, enjoy-
ing the occasional fine outlooks over Flanders Bay and

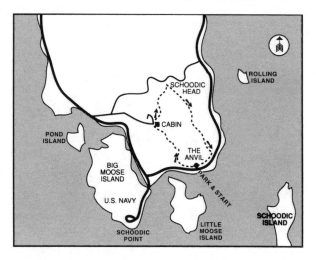

Frenchman Bay. Make a *left* and stay on ME 186 at Winter Harbor, coming shortly to the Acadia National Park service road less than a mile *east* of the village. You now turn *right* and drive farther *south*, crossing an inlet and passing Frazer Point. The road follows the east side of Frenchman Bay, where you have spectacular views to Mount Desert. Seabirds move in great clouds above the bay's choppy waters. During storms, the waves race along powerfully, crashing on the granite shore. The road arrives at a junction after passing West Pond Cove near the former U.S. Naval Reservation. Bear *left*, driving more *eastward* around the point, and watch very carefully for the Blueberry Hill turnout on your *right*. (Go slow. All traffic in this section is one-way. If you miss the trailhead, you'll have to make a complete loop around the point before reaching the trailhead again.) Leave your car at the well-marked Blueberry Hill turnout.

The route to Schoodic Head begins on the north side

of the road, opposite the Blueberry Hill parking area entrance. A small, weathered sign marks the trailhead. Walk the trail northwest on a little-used, grassy road that runs through a grove of smooth alder. The path pulls to the right at the top of the rise, running generally northward through ledgy terrain grown up in red and white spruce. A swampy area marked by a bent white paper birch is passed shortly as the trail rises slightly. After passing two wet depressions, the trail levels once more, then climbs still again through more birch and alder by a little pond. Soon you pass the warden's cabin on the right, where you proceed straight ahead on a wider, gravel road. Watch for the Schoodic Head Trail on the right a short way past the cabin and head rightward into the woods.

You now have an interesting 1-mile hike uphill to the east amid a series of boulders and groves of spruce and hemlock. Decaying logs are host to shelf fungi and haircap moss. The red-blazed trail next rises steeply through tangles of blowdown and, working northwestward, soon reaches several exposed ledges. You climb to a plateau and then rise yet more steeply through a cleft in the ledge. The route now climbs farther still, crossing a little brook and moving upward through more exposed rock and ledge.

At this altitude some of the excellent westerly views that this trail provides begin to open up. You come to ledges dotted with jack pines, where there are open vistas to the islands of Frenchman Bay. In clear weather, you can see the hills of Mount Desert. Continuing upward to the northeast and east, you walk over bare ledge and then into a protected depression. Winding its way through clumps of rhodora, the trail emerges soon on the east summit. Minutes before, your outlook was to the west, but it is now to the east. Excellent views are had over Schoodic and Wonsqueak Harbors and out to the cold, blue Atlantic beyond. (The ocean never looks warm here, even on a hot summer day. Nor is it. Fifty-five to 58 degrees is about as warm as these waters ever get. And in winter? Don't ask.)

There are alternative routes as you prepare to head downward. It is pleasant to retrace your steps over the

ledges and through the jack pines to lower ground, particularly in sunny weather when the air is dry and you
can walk down into those good views of Mount Desert.
If you want to try another way to the road, take the
Anvil Trail southeast off the summit. Dropping rather
steeply downward through more groves of jack pines,
with their weathered gray cones, this trail runs down
through some unstable scree. Watch your footing.
Sheep laurel, spruce, and ground juniper border the
path as you descend to a notch known as the Anvil. The
trail then continues east and south through further
stands of spruce. Reindeer and antler lichens flourish
in the ground cover. You come out to the park service
road about a mile below the summit. Turn right (southwest) on the paved road here, and walk back to your
car just a short distance away.

If you make the round trip via the warden's cabin
both ways, this walk is roughly 3⅔ miles. The hike can
be done in 2½ hours without rushing. If you ascend
via the warden's cabin and descend via the Anvil, the
route is about 2¾ miles and takes two hours. The
ground and ledges can be rough and sometimes slippery, so wear good hiking boots.

Once you're back down to the pavement, drive *north*
on the park road up the west side of Schoodic Harbor,
past Wonsqueak and Bunker Harbors to ME 186 in
Birch Harbor. Bear *left* on ME 186 and follow it through
Winter Harbor *west* and *north* to US 1.

43·Petit Manan Point

Location: Steuben, Maine
Distance: 3 miles
Walking time: 2 hours

Well downeast, beyond more heavily visited, fabled destinations around Bar Harbor, you find that part of the Maine coast better known to Mainers themselves. In this region Petit Manan Point lies east of Ellsworth and just south of Milbridge. A long arrowhead of land that drops into the Atlantic below Steuben, Petit Manan Point (which traces its name from the nearby island) hosts a U.S. Fish and Wildlife Service sanctuary. The walking in the refuge is quiet and secluded, more subject to wind, weather, and tides than to the motorized tourist hordes that invade the coast farther south.

The Petit Manan Wildlife Refuge is comprised of nearly 3,200 acres of coastal woodland, just under 2,000 acres of which are on Petit Manan Peninsula itself. The rest of the refuge occupies Bois Bubert Island to the east and nearby Petit Manan and Nash Islands. This cluster of refuge properties supports both native and migratory bird species numbering in the hundreds. An interpretive guide to the refuge and its wildlife, as well as other information, is available where you leave your car.

Petit Manan Point is reached via US 1 from Ellsworth or Machias. Approach the point on Pigeon Hill Road, which you will find well marked where it intersects US 1, 3 miles *northeast* of the Steuben Fire Department buildings. Drive *south* on winding Pigeon Hill Road, staying always on the main road, making no turns onto any side roads. Just under 6 miles from the highway, Pigeon Hill Road becomes gravel surfaced after passing along great open stretches of the bay, and you shortly arrive at the refuge parking area. No motorized traffic is allowed beyond this lot.

A little gem of a woods walk, this 3-mile round trip to Birch Point at the northwest corner of Petit Manan Point can be navigated by persons of any ability. An easy tramp over grassy woods roads and trails, the route to Birch Point takes the hiker to splendid outlooks over Dyer Bay up-channel from the open ocean.

The Birch Point Trail begins on the southwest side of the parking area and runs west across an old blueberry barren marked, here and there, with paths made by deer. Crossing this sere expanse of open ground, the trail arches northwest into the woods grown up in white birch, tamarack, spruce, and red maple. The path follows a grassy, rutted old tote road as it winds through thick growth punctuated by lumps of granite ledge and boulders. More birch, spotted alder, red spruce, and staghorn sumac border the path. In minutes you emerge in another blueberry field, which slopes prettily downhill toward the woods in the west.

Continuing northwestward, the path bends through some aspens, birches, and more spruce, quickly opening on another field to your right. Blueberries and wild cranberries grow in the field. This is perfect upland

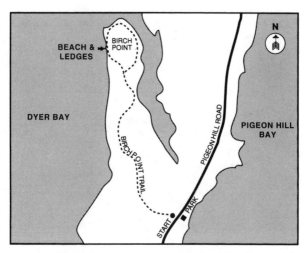

game country. In moments you are back in the woods again, where a thick stand of balsam shades the ground to your right and an open range of red maples grows to the left. Haircap mosses and clumps of bunchberry fill in the undergrowth. Here you will begin to notice the unique fragrance of these woods, especially in autumn. A pungent, sweet odor of balsam, rotting leaves, and goldenrod, together with the salt air of the nearby ocean, rises from the scrub. The trail dips northward in a row of spindly white birches and passes through a little clearing, pulling sharply westward and over a footbridge. A sheltered bog is screened by trees to the right.

Widening, the road becomes more grassy, passes some silver birches, and enters another clearing where a side trail leads right and downhill to pretty views on an inlet of Dyer Bay. Shorebirds may often be found patrolling the flats here at low tide, the bright underbellies of herring gulls brilliant against the mud. The main trail pushes on northward and detours on a

shoofly path cut through the brush, coming back out of the woods again after looping around a boggy section. You will pass a grove of cedars as the road climbs, proceeds through clumps of mountain ash and fragrant balsam, and crosses another footbridge. The brilliant red berries of the ash, though bitter, attract birds of many species. Grouse nest in the undergrowth. Black-capped chickadees flit from branch to branch.

A bit over a mile from the parking area, you descend to a trail junction at a clearing and go left and northwest on the Birch Point Trail. The route narrows to a grassy and leaf-strewn path littered with small boulders. You next come to a Birch Point Loop sign, where you head left once again and begin to walk more to the west through some spindly maples. White and silver birches, some of them large and old, grow in numbers near the end of the wooded section of the trail. A short descent west to the shore of Dyer Bay brings you into the open.

Fine views of Sally and Sheep Islands greet your

emergence onto the bayside ledges and inlets. These two islands lie immediately to the west and northwest. Around to the south, well down the bay, you can see open ocean. Plenty of opportunities exist here for southward exploration along Dyer Bay's eastern ledges. A small cove, one of a series around Birch Point, lies at the trail's end. Shoreline exploration here can be interesting, and if you desire, you can follow the path *around* the point, arriving back at the last trail junction you passed on the way in.

Whether you simply retrace your steps or head around Birch Point to the trail junction, follow the same route from the junction back to the parking area. This walk can be done (out and back) in just over two hours, but that would be needlessly rushing it. Once you've sampled these pretty woods and the exhilaration of the bay ledges on a sunny autumn day, you'll find little merit in hurrying. Add extra time to these estimates if you decide to walk the point loop before returning.

The paths of Petit Manan Point are open from April 15 to November 15. Information on the refuge and wildlife species found here can be obtained from: Manager, Moosehorn National Wildlife Refuge, Box X, Calais, ME 04619.

44· West Quoddy Head

Location: Lubec, Maine
Distance: 1 to 4 miles (depending on route
   selected)
Walking time: 1 to 3 hours

The U.S.A. doesn't go any farther east than here. Peering out over over the Grand Manan Channel, this isolated peninsula stands guard over a tough, lovely section of the North Atlantic within shouting distance of Canada. West Quoddy Head Light, a brilliantly striped presence on the outer ledges, oversees the channel, beyond which lies the misty, north–south expanse of Grand Manan, a Canadian island where the author's grandmother, Amanda Willcox Hanson, was born and raised.

Because Quoddy is home to one of the Northeast's most famous lighthouses, many visitors come to Quoddy Head each year. Only a few take time beyond visiting the lighthouse to extensively *walk* this dramatic section of the coast. The head is home to a variety of ecological features worth seeing, most of which require a walk away from the developed area near the lighthouse. Southeast of the village of Lubec, Quoddy is a flat, open, grassy neck on its landward side, which rolls up into higher, densely wooded ground to seaward. High cliffs plunge from the head's eastern side, and 20-foot-

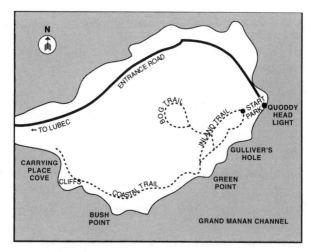

plus tides are usual. Quoddy Head belongs to the Maine Bureau of Parks and Recreation and is operated as a state park with daytime hours. Vehicle parking, maps, and other aids to visitors are available on arrival.

To reach this dramatic stretch of shore, drive *east* from US 1 on ME 189 opposite the Whiting Community Church in Whiting. Proceed toward Lubec. Before entering Lubec village, watch for a large sign marking a *right* turn 10 miles east of US 1. Turn *right* and *south*, passing through a small residential neighborhood. The road gradually pulls eastward and crosses a narrow, barren neck of land, really an emergent peat bog, and continues over a rise to the head. At the end of the road, take a *right* into the parking area.

After leaving your car, a short walk northeast from the lot will bring you to the lighthouse. This fine structure is one of that long procession of U.S. Coast Guard lighthouses converted to automated operation as a means of saving money. Local fishermen, and others who use these waters regularly, protested loudly at the conversion, for they know that a lighthouse keeper is a much more reliable implement than an electronic, solid-state, programmable beacon control.

(To be explicit, the fine men and women of the U.S. Coast Guard have been staffing lighthouses and patrolling our shores for decades, underfunded, underequipped, and under-recognized, and still they persevere. The real culprit, of course, is the U.S. Congress, which can find money for $2.25-billion throwaway space rockets, but not the small amount it would take to properly support our guardsmen and -women and their installations.)

Returning to the parking lot, you will find a large signboard indicating three major nature trails in the park. The Inland Trail carries the walker through the densely forested central grounds of Quoddy Head, introducing the attractive coniferous vegetation typical of the northern Maine coast. This trail gradually makes its way southward to the ocean at Green Point. You can retrace your steps from there or, taking the Coastal Trail, turn and follow it northeastward to the parking area. The Inland Trail provides a 2-mile round trip requiring a little over an hour, whichever route you use on the return.

The Bog Trail makes a loop around the swampy low ground in the middle of the head. This walk departs from the Inland Trail about ¾ mile west of where you parked. Those enthused about birding and wildlife will find this walk interesting. It can also be combined with the Inland-Coastal loop mentioned above to create a walk of one and a half to two hours.

Quoddy Head's longest walk, the Coastal Trail,

makes a 4-mile round trip around the southeast perimeter of the head to Carrying Place Cove and back. This trail has the best water views, following, as it does, the rocky headland overlooking the channel. On this route you pass Gulliver's Hole, Green Point, and Bush Point and reach the south side of Carrying Place Cove, site of an old herring weir and the raised peat upland mentioned earlier.

If you want to combine these paths into a long, continuous hike that will take up most of a glorious day's walking, do this. On the outward leg, walk the full length of the Coastal Trail to Carrying Place Cove, enjoying the marvelous seaward views along the way. Have lunch at the cove, then walk back to Green Point, turning west on the Inland Trail. When you come to the Bog Trail, bear left and west onto it. Emerging from the Bog Trail, follow the Inland Trail left and north to your car.

Remember that the park is open for day use and that the gates are shut at dusk.

Index